Youth Basketball Drills & Plays Handbook

By Bob Swope
1st Edition 2007
2nd Edition 2008

"If you liked this book and you think that it helped you and your team or parents and their children, tell all your friends and family about it."

Published and Distributed By:
Jacobob Press LLC
St. Louis, MO.
(314) 843-4829

ISBN 10 0-9820960-3-8
ISBN 13   978-0-9820960-3-1
SAN 257-1862

Printed and Bound by:
No Waste Publishing
Fenton, MO.

Second Edition 2008

*******WARNING********

If your child or the participant has any physically limiting condition, bleeding disorder, high blood pressure, pregnancy or any other condition that may limit them physically you should check with your doctor before letting them participate in any of these, drills or plays.

Be sure participants, in these drills and plays that might make hard contact with any of the other participants are all approximately of the same weight and size to avoid a possible injury.

All the drills and plays for kids, should be supervised by an adult, coach, or a professional. **AUTHOR ASSUMES NO LIABILITY FOR ANY ACCIDENTAL INJURY OR EVEN DEATH THAT MAY RESULT.**

Extra care and caution should be taken with any of the various passing drills or plays, and some dribbling drills and plays as they are the more dangerous ones.

Bob Swope
Jacobob Press LLC
Publisher

TABLE OF CONTENTS

Introduction

Intent

Many youth coaches have asked me about easily identified offensive and defensive plays and drills they can use. This book is intended to be a supplemental book to my "Teach'n Basketball" book. It is oriented more towards team coaches on youth teams rather than parents at home teaching fundamentals. We will break this down into what they are doing at the time and what plays to use that will accomplish your goals. My suggestion is, use the time you have each weak to maximize what you want to teach. For little kids it's better to break practice drills down into more than one small group.

Training Sessions

Then keep the group training to 15 minute sessions, blow your whistle, and rotate the kids from one group to the next group. In other words always keep all your kids busy doing something at all times except for water breaks. Don't have any kids just standing around waiting. You get more teaching in this way, the kids don't get bored, and they learn more this way. Get as many assistant coaches as they will let you have, then explain to them what you want each one to teach at their group station. Time wise plan your whole practice session. The kids will then learn more in the short period of time you have for teaching each week.

The opponent

It's probably smart to try and understand what the teams you play against are doing against you offensively and defensively. Especially after you have played them once you should have a good idea. Keep a small pad of paper in your pocket and take notes. Then what you want to do for a game plan is, pick the offense or defense that will counter, and defeat, what they are doing. Have a game plan before you go into a game, and make sure all your coaches and kids know what it is. Also have a back up plan just in case your game plan is not working like you expected.

Drills

I am going to refer to the drills as "Skill Training Activities" because that's what they really are. Also I am going to throw in a term now being used a lot. It is called "Core Training". What it does is train their body to make certain moves that will make them a better Basketball player. Skill activities will be organized by *"numbers"* so that you can have your assistant coaches use them and become more familiar with them that way.

Plays

For easy reference the plays will be organized by *"numbers"* also. They will be arranged as Offensive and Defensive plays. The legend page will show you the symbols for player movement, passing, screening, dribbling, and new location moving for clarification. Each play will have a short explanation for how it is supposed to work, strong points, and what it is designed to accomplish.

Strategies

The first strategy I recommend is "have a game plan" to match the team you are playing. Remember though these are only kids, so coach accordingly with your strategies. You know the old "KISS" (Keep-It-Simple-Stupid) phrase. Here are some you can use:

For Offense

1. If you have a big tall center, and the other team does not, then put your center near the basket in the lo- post, and get the ball to them. Teach them to jump *way up* when they shoot, they may make the basket, and draw some fouls that way.
2. If you have one of the faster teams in your division, then use a fast break, or a motion offense.
3. If your team is good at ball handling, then you can use just about any of the offenses, depending on who you are playing, and what their strengths are.

For Defense

1. If the other team has one big high scoring forward, use a "box and one" defense. Use your best guard to pressure their dominate center, but remind them to work at not fouling the center. Play the ball and not the player.
2. If your opponent is penetrating your team to the basket, without much opposition, use the "triangle and two" defense.
3. Also if your opponent is penetrating a lot and getting in close to the basket for shots, you can use a "1-3-1 Zone" to force them to take more long corner shots which will be harder for them to make.
4. If your team has more talented players than your opponent, you could play a straight up "man to man" defense. You probably will not have much trouble as long as you match up evenly with their players. By that I mean use your fast guards on their guards, and your tallest player on their center. Fast small guards will get around a big slow center.
5. If you have a big center and two big forwards, you can use a "2-3 Zone "defense quite effectively. To form a block out line to keep their small players from penetrating, the key player is your center that has to seal off any players that break through your forwards. If the opponent gets their shot off, teach your center to "box out", and "rebound". See more discussion on this in the **"Teach'n Basketball"** book.
6. If your players are mostly big tall and slower, do not press when the other team takes the ball out at their end of the court. Especially if your opponent is smaller and faster because it will make it easier for them to fast break around your player standing in front of their player taking the ball out.

Legend for Diagrams

$\otimes$ = INSTRUCTOR OR COACH

[X] = DEFENSIVE PLAYERS

■X■ = OFFENSIVE PLAYERS

———┤ = DEFENSIVE PLAYER MOVEMENT

———▶ = OFFENSIVE PLAYER MOVEMENT

----▶ = BALL MOVEMENT OR PASSES

———▶┤ = OFFENSIVE MOVEMENT WITH SCREEN

⌒○ = ARM AND HAND POSITION

〰〰 = DRIBBLING

X = LOCATION A PLAYER IS MOVING TO OR FROM

NO. 1 & 2 ARE GUARDS, NO. 3 & 4 ARE
FORWARDS, NO. 5 IS THE CENTER

Offensive Plays

There are not nearly as many offensive basketball plays as there are say football plays. But there are certain basic alignment plays, man to man plays, and zone plays, a team can run to defeat a particular defense, or an offense.

Simple Basic Offensive Plays

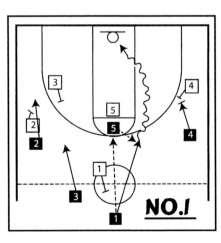

Give & Go (No.1)

Get all your players, except No.4, quickly up court. Try to get the opposition to think you are moving towards the left corner. Have your No.4 player get the oppositions No. 4 player to follow them to the right corner of the court. When that starts to happen, have your No.1 player pass the ball to your No.5 player at the top of the key (the Give), who then fakes turning to their right, then turns back to their left and passes back to No. 1 breaking up court past them as they go by. No.1 then goes directly to the basket for a lay-up (the Go). You can also flip flop, or go the opposite way, with this same play.

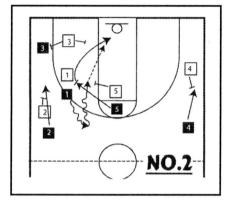

Pick & Roll (No.2)

Your player No.1 gets the ball to the left of the lane, then starts to dribble toward the top of the key. At that same time your player No.5 moves over to screen out the oppositions player No.1 (the PICK). Then player No. 1 can do several things. If they are clear to go around the screen, and past the oppositions player No.5, then they dribble to the basket for a lay-up. If the oppositions No.5 comes over to seal them off from the basket, then your player No.5 rolls and breaks to the basket (the ROLL). Your No.1 bounce passes them the ball for a lay up. If both the oppositions players No.1 and 5 go to seal off No.1, they still pass to No. 5 for a lay-up.

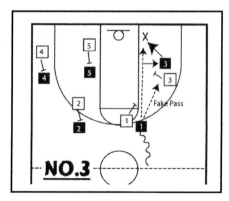

The Back Door (No.3)

If your team is bigger, but slow, this could work for you against an aggressive team that overplays the passing lanes. This play is designed to go to your player No.3 around the "back door" as they call it. First your No. 1 player dribbles up into the front court to the top of the 3 point arc. Player No.3 steps to the right side, behind the opposing player No.3. Then your No.1 fakes a pass to your No.3 player. If the opposing No.3 player steps in front

10

to block the pass, your No.3 player then turns and goes to the basket for the back door pass lay up. This works best when your No.3 player gets behind the opposing No.3 player.

The Pass and Screen Away (No.4)

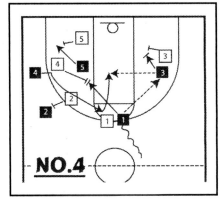

In this play your No.1 player brings the ball up to the top of the key. They then pass the ball to your No.3 player. At the same time your No.4 player moves in a zigzag zag towards the top of the key, right at your No.1. They pass each other, and as the oppositions No.4 tries to follow your No.4 player, your No.1 player blocks out and screens them. This should free up your No.4 player to get a pass back from No.3 as they break towards the basket for a lay up. Then your No.3 screens out their No.3, hopefully leaving the lane free. This will only work if you can get the opposing team to overload the left side of the court.

Zone Offensive Plays

1-3-1 Zone Cutter (No.5)

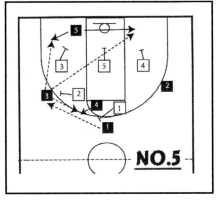

This is a basic play against a 2-3 Zone Defense. Your No.1 player brings the ball up into the front court, to the top of the key. Then they turn and pass to your No.3 player. Your No.3 player then becomes the play maker. They have several options, they can look for your No.5 player as a cutter, either way, on the base line and pass to them, or they can pass to your No.4 breaking into a clear space on the perimeter. This is an overload to the left side play. You can also flip flop it, and overload to the right.

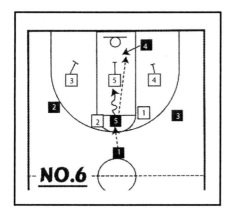

1-3-1 Zone Turn or Fill (No.6)

This is another basic play against a 2-3 Zone Defense. This play probably works best when you have a fairly big center who is a good shooter. Your No.1 player brings the ball up towards the front court. Then they pass the ball to your No.5 center on the hi post. Your No.5 center immediately pivots all the way around and faces the basket. If they have space in front of them, they dribble a few steps then take a jump shot at the basket. If your opponents No.5 player starts to come in and collapse on them, they pass to your No. 4 player, who has filled into the lane behind their No.5 under the basket.

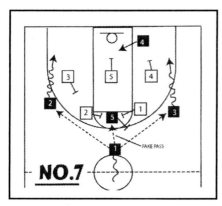

1-3-1 Zone Wings Free (No.7)

Here is still another play against a 2-3 Zone Defense. This play works by putting your No.5 center at the hi post. Your No.1 player brings the ball up towards the front court. Then they fake a pass to your No.5 center, which usually causes the defense to collapse on your center. After that your center moves to their left. The zone players should rotate around to the right side to follow your center. Your No.1 player then looks to see if your No. 3 player is clear. That look should rotate the zone even more to the right side. Then your No.1 turns and passes to your No. 2 player, who should be open to go to the basket.

1-2-2 Zone Across Court (No.8)

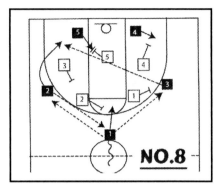

This play can easily shift from a 1-3-1 offense to this 1-2-2 offense. In this case we are showing it against a 2-3 Zone Defense, which is popular for many youth teams to use. Your No.1 player brings the ball up into the front court. Then your No.1 player passes the ball to your No.2 player out on the left wing. This should cause the zone to rotate over to the left side a little. Next your No.2 player passes the ball right back to your No.1 player. Your No.1 player then passes the ball to your No.3 player on the right wing. The opponents zone players then think you are trying to trick them, and they will probably rotate back to the right side. As soon as your No.3 player can see that is happening, they make a long over the top pass back to your No.2 player that has slipped in behind the zone. They take it to the basket or make a short jump shot. Your No.5 moves in and screens out their No.5 or No.3 player, whichever is closest to the basket.

1-2-2 Zone Moving Screen (No.9)

This play is shown against a 2-3 zone defense. First your No.1 player brings the ball up in the front court. Next they dribble toward your No.3 player on the right wing. Your No.3 fakes getting the pass, and then breaks up across the lane and screens out the opponents No. 5 or No. 3, whichever is

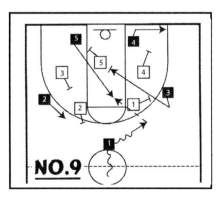

13

closest to the center of the lane. As soon as your No.1 dribbles toward your No.3, your No.5 player breaks toward the top of the lane. As soon as they get there your No.1 passes them the ball, they stop and make a quick turnaround jumper shot at the basket. Your No.4 moves way out on the base line forcing their No. 4 to go out to guard them. Their No.1 and No.2 players should be too far away to make a play on your No.5. This play has to be run very fast though so there is not a "too much time in the lane" violation. Your key players (No.3 & No. 5) have to be very good at reading the defense, to make this play work.

1-2-2 Moving Screen Option

This play combines the two previous plays (across court & moving screen), and turns them into 2 options.

The First Option (No.10) is:

After seeing the other two plays, the defense will think it's the same play coming again, and being kids they can get really

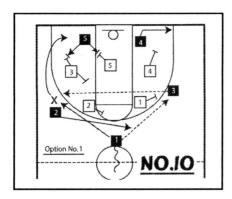

Option No.1

NO.10

confused. Your No.1 brings the ball up into the front court. Then instead of faking a pass to your No.3 player, they pass the ball to your No.3. At the same time your No.5 player starts to move to the top of the key, but then stops and screens the opponents No.5 player. If the opponents No.3 bites on the pass to your No.3, and rotates towards the right side, this should get your No.1 free on the left wing for a cross court pass. Your No.2 moves to the right wing area. No.1 should then be able to move around your No.5's screen, and go for a short jump shot or a lay up.

The Second Option (No.11) is:

If your No.3 player can see that your No.1, who has moved to the left wing, is covered for a cross court pass, they pass to your

14

No.2. When the defense can see the pass is back to the top of the key, they will probably rotate towards that area, and away from your No.1 player. At that point your No. 2 quick passes over to your No.1. Then your No.2 breaks for the right wing area, and gets a pass back across court from your

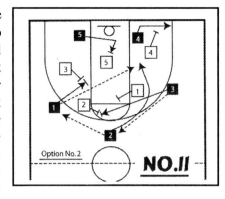

No.1. If your No.4 player has decoyed the oppositions No.4 player way over on the base line with them, then the right wing area should be free for your No.2 to go for a jump shot or a lay up. During this time your No.5 player has to time a screen, on the oppositions No.5 player, for your No.2 to make the basket. Watch for too much time in the lane. Your No.1 then screens out their No.3.

Motion Offensive Plays

You must have a fast energetic team to run motion plays. Your players will have to move a lot, pass a lot, screen a lot, and block a lot. If you are going to run these plays, I suggest you first make sure all your players know the fundamentals of, moving without the ball, quick passing, screening out, and how to correctly block the opponent. If they can't apply these fundamentals, you are going to get a lot of fouls called.

The Arrow

This starts out as a 1-2-2 offensive set.

For the first motion (No.12)

Your No.1 brings the ball up into the front court. Your player No.2 moves up towards the ball. Your No.4 player breaks from the hi- post across the

lane down to the left side of the key. Your No.3 turns toward the lane and screens their No.1 until your No. 4 player starts to get through the lane. Then they have to move quickly to the hi-post, on the right side.

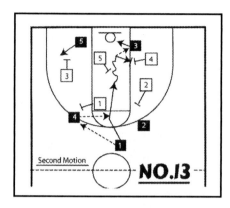

Second Motion

NO.13

For the second motion (No.13)

Your No.1 passes the ball to your No.4, then breaks up the lane towards the basket. If it's open your No.1 and No.4 work a "give and Go". Then your No.1 dribbles up the lane toward the basket, turns to the right and passes the ball to your No.3. Next No. 1 screens for No.3, who breaks for the basket and makes a lay up or a short jump shot. Your No.5 moves out to the edge of the 3 point circle, hopefully pulling their No.3 player with them.

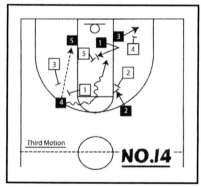

Third Motion

NO.14

For the third motion (No.14)

If your No.4 can't work the "give and go" with No.1, they can pass to your No.5, who has moved back over to the edge of the lane. Or if it's open they can follow your No.1 up the lane, and right to the basket. The desired option is to pass to your No.5 player, who is in a better position to go to the basket for a lay up or a jump shot. Your No.1 must get out of the lane before too much time in the lane is called, then quickly move back across the lane to screen out their No. 5 player. If your No. 4 dribbles up the middle, your No.2 has to screen out their No. 2.

For the fourth motion (No.15)

If your No.5 can not get open for a shot, they hold the ball. In the mean time, your No.3 has cut back across the lane and curled

16

to the other side, way out on the edge of the 3 point arc as a safety valve. If your No.4 did not dribble up the middle, they fake a cut toward the middle of the lane, and then move back out to the point on the 3 point arc. At this point, your No.5 has to take a shot or pass out to your No.3 or No.4 players. When your No.1 and

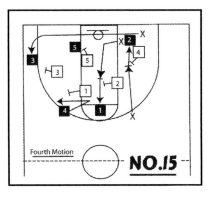

Fourth Motion

NO.15

No.2 players see your No.5 is jammed up and stalling, they pick for each other with No.1 moving down to the free throw line, and No.2 executing a "back door" moving to the lo post. No.2 should be open for a jump shot or a lay up, if so your No.5 passes them the ball. At this point if none of this works, your No.5 passes back out to your No.1 at the free throw line, to reload.

Overload Back Cut

This starts out as a 1-3-1 offensive set.

For the first motion (No.16):

This play works when you notice the defense is overloading on you to one side. If the defense is overloaded to the other side, everything is just flip flopped. Your No.1

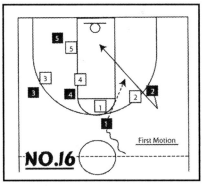

First Motion

NO.16

brings the ball up into the front court. Your No.5 has to do some acting, to get the opponents No.5 to go way over to the left to guard them. When your No.2 can see this happen, and recognizes there is open space to the basket, they quickly take a step or two back towards center court as if they will get a pass from your No.1. Then they pivot, turn, and cut (flash) to the basket for a lay up or a short jumper.

For the second motion (No.17)

If your No.2 player can see the defense has shifted more to the center, and they can't flash to the basket, they delay their flash.

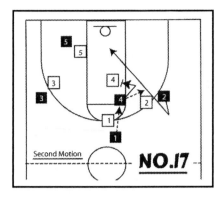

Second Motion

NO.17

When your No.4 can see No.2 is holding, they quickly move to the other side of the free throw line. Your No.1 then passes them the ball. When your No.2 can see the pass going to No.4, they quickly fake moving back, then flash to the basket. Your No.4 does a "give and go" with them as they go by. If your No.5 has made their decoy, No.2 takes it to the basket for a lay up or a short jumper. Your No.4 screens for your No.2.

For the third motion (No.18)

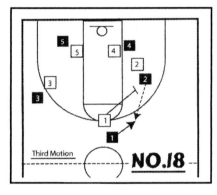

Third Motion

NO.18

If your No.2 gets the ball, and they can see they are about to be double teamed, they stop and kick (pass) the ball back out to your No.1. Your No.1 upon noticing No.2 is about to get double teamed, moves to a clear space on the right wing. When your No.1 gets the ball they can shoot a 3 point shot, or move in closer to the basket for a jump shot. If none of this works, then your No.1 moves back out to the 3 point circle and reloads the offense.

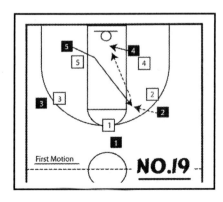

First Motion

NO.19

Hi-Lo Post Motion

This starts out as a 1-2-2 offensive set.

For the first motion (No.19)

This offense is for 2 good lo-post players working together. It is shown against a 3-2 Zone defense, or a man to man defense. If your No. 4 lo-post is being fronted by a defensive player, your No.5

18

lo-post player flashes across court to the right side of the free throw line. When your No.4 lo-post player can see that No. 5 is getting the pass from your No.2, they break towards the basket, and get the pass from your No.5 to go in for the lay up.

For the second motion (No.20)
        If your No.4 lo-post has the defensive player behind them, your No. 2 player passes the ball to your No.4. At the same time your No.5 player breaks and moves down to the left side of the free throw line, hopefully pulling the

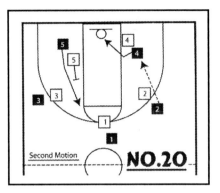

oppositions No. 5 player with them. When your No. 4 player can see the oppositions No.5 player move down, they do a hook step and move around the player guarding them, and go to the basket for a lay up, or a reverse lay up.

For the third motion (No.21)
        If your No.4 players defender has their hand in front of your No.4, your No.2 player holds the ball and waits for your No.5 to get clear into the lane. When your No.4 can see that they can't get the pass for a lay up, they break across court and screen the oppositions No.5 player.

When your No.5 player can see this happening, they break down and across into the lane for a pass. If they are clear, they turn and make a jump shot at the basket.

For the fourth motion (No.22)
        If their No.4 and No. 5 defenders do a switch, then your No.5 player should move on over to the right side corner, pulling

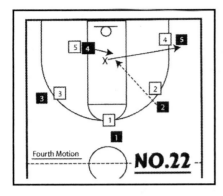

their defender with them. Next when your No.4 player observes all of this happening, they do a turn around sealing off their defender, and break towards the middle of the lane for a pass. Your No.2 then passes them the ball, and they turn to their left for a lay up or a jump shot.

Transition Offensive Plays

Your transition offense can be "fast break", or a "walk it up the floor" transition. The fast break can produce easy scores. Moving it up the floor quickly puts a lot of pressure on the defense. To run it you need a fast energetic team. The up tempo game should favor the team that is well conditioned. A team that is maybe bigger and heavier, and not well conditioned, will "run out of gas" so to speak by the third or fourth quarter. If you have a lot of good fast bench players on your team, it is in your advantage to use the up tempo game. Also getting the ball up the floor quickly before the defense can get set, works good against Zone Defenses. If your team is bigger and slower, then it's in your advantage to walk or bring the ball up court more slowly and methodically.

On transitions, have your post players get up the floor quickly when possible, with a guard that is a good ball handler bringing it up the court in back. This leaves room for the guards to maneuver, or maybe throw a long pass if the post player beats the defense up court.

Primary fast Break Transition (No.23)

One of the best ways to run the fast break is, teach your players that there are 3 lanes to come up the court in. One lane is up the middle, and the other two are along the sidelines. The idea is to fill all 3 lanes, not just one or two, as you come up the floor. And as they come up the floor, there is a "trailer" (No.4) and a "prevent" player (No.5). Actually it doesn't matter which 3 players is in which lane up front, just as long as they spread out and fill all 3 lanes as quickly as they can, then GO fast. Usually the "trailer", and the "prevent" player, is designated so they know the role they play.

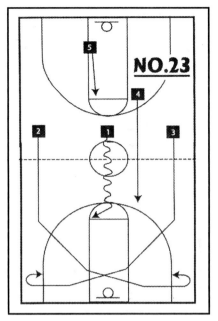

NO.23

When it's an outlet play, most coaches say have the outlet pass go to the point guard (No.1). When the outlet pass is after a score, make sure your No.1 is in the middle area of the court to take the pass. When the outlet pass is from a sideline, make sure your No.1 goes to that sideline quickly to take the pass. After your No.1 has received the pass, they dribble and move quickly to the center lane, then come up the court. And if the fast break does not develop, they slow down and bring the ball up slowly to avoid a turnover.

On defensive rebounds, the general rule is the player that gets the rebound is the last player to come up the court. First thing they do is, get the ball to your No.1 in the middle of the court. This is the fastest, easiest, and safest way to get the fast break going. Your No.1 should dribble all the way up to the top of the key before making a pass if possible. The 2 outside lane players cut across the court at 45 degrees (criss cross), and look for a pass from your No.1. If your No.1 stops and makes a jump shot from around the free throw line, the 2 wing players should crash the board for a rebound. The "prevent" player comes up the court slowly, their job is make sure no opponent player gets behind them. That way if an opponent intercepts or steals the ball, they don't have a clear path to the basket. If the fast break does not develop, your No.1 waits for everyone to get up the court, then sets up your half court offense. Most coaches say a successful fast break depends on:

1. Make sure you get the defensive rebound.
2. An accurate, quick outlet pass.

3. Fill all 3 lanes quickly.
4. Stay in control. You should be quick, but never hurry.
5. Be alert visually. Don't force the break, or make a bad pass if the players are not in position to make it work.

There are some "special situations" to make your players aware of in the primary fast break.

First Option   NO.24

Second Option   NO.25

First Option   NO.26

The 2 on 1 Fast Break

The *first option* (No.24) is, when your No.1 finds a "2 on 1" fast break situation, they should take the ball directly to the basket, or get fouled. They should try to attack the basket at an angle, from along the lane line. Their No.2 team mate should take a position on the opposite side, at the lo-post, and watch for a pass or the rebound.

The *second option* (No.25) is, when your No.1 can see that the defender has come up and is blocking their path to the basket and ready to take a "charging" foul, they pull up and pass to the team mate (No.2), who takes it quickly to the basket for a lay up.

The 3 on 2 Fast Break

The *first option* (No.26) is, see where the defenders are set up as you approach the top of the key. As you are coming down the middle of the court, usually one defender will try to stop you at the free throw line. And the second defender will probably be positioned down low right under the basket. If that is the case, your No.1 should not penetrate beyond the free throw line. They stop there and look for either your No.2 or No.3 players driving to the basket. They pass to whichever player is most open. That player tries to dribbles to the basket for a lay up. At this point it is a 2 on 1 situation with the opponents No.3 player. If their No.3 player moves to block your No. 2 player, they pass over to your No.3 player for the lay up.

The *second option* (No.27) is, if your No.2 player starts to dribble to the basket, and is blocked by their No.3 who has moved over, they either pass to your No.3 on the other side of the lane or back to your No. 1. If they pass off to your No.1, then No.1 immediately breaks toward  the basket for a lay up. If the opponents No.1 moves to a position to block your No.1, they can pass to your No.3 for the lay up.

Secondary Fast Break Transition

When a primary fast break is not an option, then run a "secondary fast break". When you have a secondary fast break play, it helps a lot in getting quick baskets in transition.

Motion Secondary Break

This is a little different type of fast break to use when your players get into the front court. Even if the defense gets back quickly, this gives you some good scoring chances.

Motion No.1 (No.28)

The inbounds pass should go quickly to your No.1 player. Your No.2 and No.3 players both sprint down the sidelines while looking for a quick pass if they are open. In this secondary break play, your No.1 should try to get the pass to either wing player

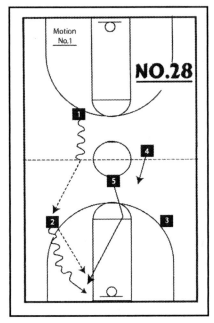

(No.2 or No.3) as soon as possible, preferably to No.2 on the strong side. This is because if the defense does not get back in time, they may be able to go in towards the basket for a lay up. Your No.5 moves down to the strong side lo-post. Your No.4 moves to the top of the arc on the opposite side from your No.1. If your No.2 can see your No.5 breaking into the clear for a lay up, they pass them the ball. Otherwise they try to flash to the basket for a lay up, or jump shot.

Motion No.2 (No.29)

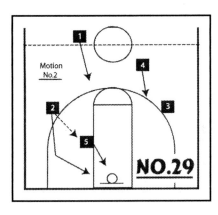

If your No.2 has a defender between them and the basket, they pass the ball to your No.5. Your No.5 can then turn around and make a turnaround jump shot, or dribble the ball in for a lay up. Your No.2 then needs to follow their pass in, around back-door, for a possible rebound.

Motion No.3 (No.30)

If your No.5 is not open, then your No.2 quickly passes the ball back out to your No.1. Then your No.1 quickly passes over to your No.4. While this is going on, your No.5 moves outside and sets a screen for No.2. Your No.2 immediately fakes going back-door to the basket, then cuts around the screen towards the middle of the lane, and looks for a pass. After screening out, Your No. 5 cuts back in towards the edge of the lane and tries to get clear for a pass.

Motion No.4 (No.31)

If the pass to your No.2 is not clear, then your No.4 holds the ball and waits for your No.2 to quickly move out to the 3 point arc for a shot. When your No.3 can see that your No.2 is moving out to the 3 point arc, they move in and screen out for them. At that point your No.4 passes the ball to your No.2, who can try for a 3 point shot.

Motion No.5 (No.32)

Just as your No.2 gets the pass from your No.4, Your No.5 player pulls their defender with them towards the free throw line elbow. Next your No.3 player sets a back screen for your No.5, who cuts back toward the basket off the screen. As they get close to the basket, your No.5 looks for a pass from your No.2, then they take it in for a lay up or a short jump shot.

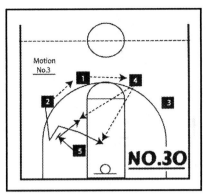

Motion No. 6 (No.33)

If your No.5 player is covered and not in the clear for a pass, your No.2 can pass the ball back out to your No.4 player, to reload and set up a hi-lo series play. This is where your No.4 shoots a 3 point shot or a jumper. Or they pass it into your No.5 player on

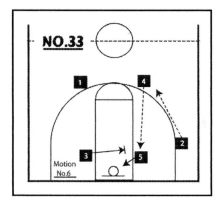

the lo-post, who hooks their defender and goes to the basket. As soon as your No.3 can see the ball is coming in to No.5, they quickly come across and screen for No.5.

Motion No. 7 (No.34)

If the hi-lo option is not open, then your No.2 holds the ball, and your No.3 moves out to the 3 point circle corner. Now you are reloaded to run "4 out- 1 in", Lo- post set plays.

Motion No.8 (No.35)

Or your No.2 can hold onto the ball while your No.1 moves over to the other side of the 3 point circle. Your No. 4 player screens for No.1, then moves down to the lo-post to block or screen for your No. 3 player. As soon as your No.4 player gets almost to the lo- post, your No.3 player moves out to the 3 point circle. Now you are reloaded to run "2 in - 3 out", set plays.

Transition after the Opponent Scores

This is a secondary break to transition after the opponent has just scored. This can work off a rebound, a steal, or it can be used to break the press. The idea is to get the ball up the court as quickly as you can.

26

Out of Bounds No.3

For Motion No.1 (No.36)
First your No.3 player has to get the ball out of the net quickly, then goes to the base line for an out of bounds pass to your No.1. Your No.2, No.4, and No.5, players quickly sprint up the court into the front court. Any passes have to be under control, and not forced. Your No.1 gets the ball and dribbles up the court. Your No.2 player sprints to the right corner of the front court. Your No.5 player sprints to the left lo-post. Your No.4 player runs fast to the left top of the key.

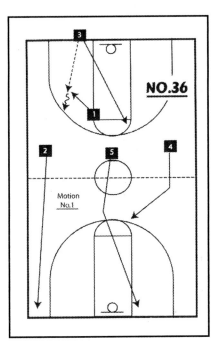

For Motion No.2 (No.37)
Your No.1 player dribbles the ball up to the front court, with your No.3 following as a "trailer". If it's open at this point, No.1 can make a long pass to your No.2 in the right corner, or to your No.5 in the lo-post. Your No.4 player holds at the left 3 point circle. Or your No.1 can dribble up into the right top of the 3 point circle.

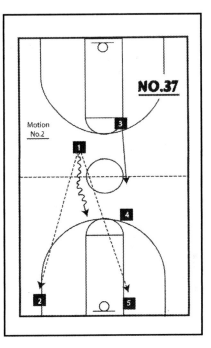

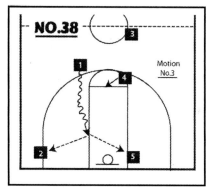

For Motion No.3 (No.38)

Your No.1 now checks the defense, and if they see an opening to the basket, then they dribble all the way to basket and attempt to score. If a defender steps in front of them, they can pass off to your No.2 or No.5 whichever is open. Your No.4 watches your No.1 dribble to the basket, and if they see No.1 start to take the shot, then they follow them in to the basket and look for the rebound.

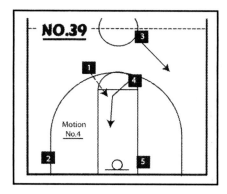

For Motion No.4 (No.39)

However if your No.1 does not see an opening to basket, and stops at the free throw line, then your No.4 makes a fast cut (flash) to the ball side of the free throw line. As they go by they look for a pass from your No.1, and they try to take it to the basket.
Your No.3 then moves to the left wing area to fill in.

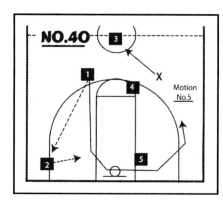

For Motion No.5 (No.40)

Another option for your No.1 is to do a "give and Go" with your No.2. To do this your No.1 passes the ball to your No.2, then breaks for the basket and looks for a pass from your No.2. passes the ball to No.1 as they go by if they are clear of a defender. If the pass is not open for No.1,

28

they cut on through and go to the left wing area. Your No.3 goes to the center of the court as a "prevent" player.

Motion No.6 (No.41)
If the pass to your No.1 is not open, your No.3 moves to the top right side of the 3 point circle, and looks for a pass from your No.2. From there if it's open, your No.3 takes a 3 point shot at the basket. Your No.4 then cuts across (flashes) down to the lo-post on the right side, and looks

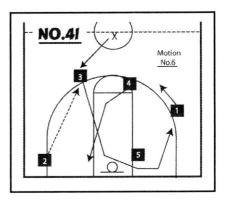

for any rebounds. If the 3 point shot does not develop, then No.3 holds at the 3 point circle. Your No.1 moves on around to the spot vacated by your No.4. Now you are reloaded, and ready for a "3 out - 2 in" set play.

Out of Bounds Offensive Plays

Your "out of bounds" plays can be quick or slow, depending on what type of players you have, and what you want to do. Some coaches like to fast break off the out of bounds, and some don't. If you notice the defenders are not getting back on defense very quick, then you can probably run a fast break. If the defenders are getting back quickly, then it's probably best to slow it down and set up a play. Less chance of a turnover. Signal with your fingers or Yell" out what you want them to do.

Quick out after a Score (No.42)
This is a play to catch the opposition off guard. It can be run off a basket, a made free throw, or a rebound. For 12 year old and up teams, you can probably only run this play several times a game to fool them. Maybe you can save this play for near the end of the game when you really need a score badly. Your No.4 and

No.5 players have to be around the basket or at the lo-post. This is basically a screen for your No.5, to get them down court quickly. Remember though you have to have a center that can run fast to make this play work. Right after the ball goes through the basket, your No.4 player grabs the ball and takes it out quickly at the base line. Your No.5 sprints down across the court towards the left wing area. Your No.2 player moves over to screen the oppositions lo-post player, just long enough so that No.5 is free to sprint down court quickly. Your No.3 player moves back up to just over mid court, then gets a long pass from your No.4 back at the base line. Then as your No.5 sprints by, they give them a little "give and go" type pass. Then No.3 turns and does a backside screen for any trailing opposition players. Your No.1 player runs down court, to fill the lane along the right side of the front court.

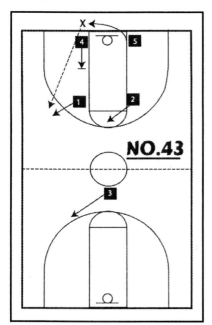

Normal End Line Out of Bounds (No.43)

This is your normal base line "out of bounds" play that can be run off a basket, a made free throw, or a rebound. If you decide you want to go down the right side of the court with the play (shown), then your first rebound position on the left side takes the ball out of the net and goes right to the end line. If you decide to go down the left side of the court, then your first rebound position on the right side takes the ball out of the net and to the end line. Some coaches give numbers to these plays, to signal their players which side they want them to go down. Whichever side the attack is designated for, the last player back will go up and fill the outside lane on the opposite side. Players No.1 and No.2 will fill the outside and middle lanes on the attack side. Your No.3 moves to fill the right side lane. Your No. 5 throws the ball in to your No.1, who moves the ball down the right side of the court. No.4 and No.5 are the "trailer" players on the play.

The Argentina

This is a base line out of bounds play, for the offensive end of the court around your basket, to free up your guard (best outside shooter) for a longer shot out on the wing. There are 2 motions to the play, one if the shot is open, and the other if it's not open.

For Motion No.1 (No.44)

Your No. 3 player takes the ball out of bounds at the base line. Your No.2 and No.5 players stack up, at the lo-post. Your No.1 player goes to the opposite lo-post from No.2 and No.5. Your No.4 player is out at the free throw line. All of a sudden your No.1 breaks straight across the lane between your No. 2 and No.5

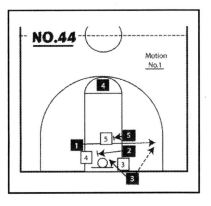

players out to the left wing area where they get a pass from your No.3 at the base line. At the same time No.1 breaks, your No.2 and No.5 players move straight ahead and double screen for No.1 to get them through and into the open. If it's open, your No.1 gets the pass, then turns around and takes a jump shot at the basket.

For Motion No.2 (No.45)

If your No.1 is not open for the shot out on the wing, then your No.3 comes over and screens out for your No.1. No.4, seeing

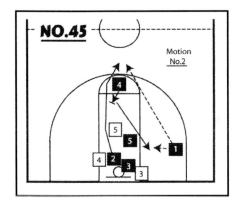

No.1 can't take the shot, moves forward and screens for No.2, who moves around No.5 to get to the top of the 3 point circle. No.4, after setting the screen, moves down and around No.5 to the left lo-post. No.1 looks at No.2 out on the 3 point circle, then at No.4 at the low post to see who is open, then whichever is most open gets the pass. No.5 just stays where they are and screens out on the backside of the play. The one big problem with this play is, your players in the lane have to be careful not to get "too long in the lane called on them. I suspect they may have to count in "1000's" to the allotted time, then all break to get out of the lane, and not get the penalty called.

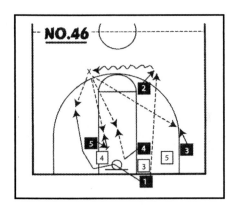

The Base line Scatter (No.46)

This is a base line play with a lot of motion to confuse the defense. Your No.1 takes the ball out at the base line. Your No.2 kind of jumps backward out towards the 3 point circle and gets a bounce pass from No.1. No.2 then dribbles over to the right side top of the key, then looks to make a pass to whoever is most open. Your No.1 after making the out of bounds pass, moves under the basket and around to the right wing area and looks for a pass from your No.2 player. No.1 is the main target for the pass and the shot. Your No.5 screens in towards the basket for your No.1, then opens up towards the free throw line, and looks back, to be open for a pass in case your No.1 is covered and doesn't get the pass. If the defense drops back there is an option to pass over to your No. 3 out on the left wing for a long shot.

Your No.4 fakes going to the basket, then steps back to the middle of the lane and looks for a pass. If they get the pass, they can make a turn around jumper to score. This is an awful lot of motion for the little kids, but it's very confusing for the defense, and might work for you with lots of practice.

The Base line Stack (No.47)

This is the old "bread and butter" out of bounds play that I see almost all the youth teams using. Your No.1 takes the ball out at the base line. Your No.2, 3, 4, and 5, stack up along the edge of the lane. The variation I see some teams using is, they

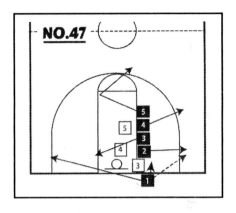

break in different directions off the basic stack. Your No.1 holds up one or two fingers, to designate which direction to go in.

On the basic stack, your No.2 is closest to the base line, then No.3 behind them, then No.4, and last No.5. Next your No.1 yells "BREAK". Then your No.5 breaks first towards the right elbow of the lane, then turns and reverses direction and goes to the top of the 3 point circle, next No.4 breaks to the left side 3 point circle. Your No.3 breaks next to the right lo post, and last your No. 2 breaks toward the left side 3 point circle. All the breaks should be in a quick sequence, one after the other. Have your players count by 1000's. No.1 looks to see who is most open, and passes them the ball. Your No.1 can then step right in to the left lo-post and fill the void left by No.2, or they break to the right side 3 point circle.

There can be all kinds of variations to the stack. I guess this is why so many teams use it, it's basic and pretty easy to teach. As an example, you can change the order of the players, from the base line out to the free throw line. Or you can change the direction each player breaks towards, to fool the defense. If you always break the same way each time, the defense will figure out how to defend against you. And maybe even get a steal or a turnover.

33

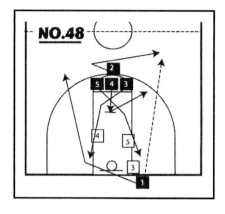

Base Line Back Stack (No.48)

This is a play that can work for the older kids, 12 years old and up. This can work especially if your team is having problems taking the ball out and getting it back in. This play works best against a zone defense. These stack plays should work with the breaks coming in quick, one after the other sequence. Have your players count by 1000's after they hear "BREAK", then break when their number comes up. Your No.1 takes the ball out at the base line. Then they yell "BREAK". Your No.4 moves first towards the basket, then sets a screen for your No.3 and No.5 players. They screen the defender in front of them, or the closest. Then No.4 holds the screen as long as they can. Your No.3 and No.5 players break together, do a "criss cross" around the screen, then head for the lo-post on each side. To make this work, your No.4 has to be a physically strong player. After your No.3 and No.5 players have cleared the screen, No.4 moves out to the 3 point circle. Your No.2 player is the safety valve option, they fake to their right, then move out to the left wing area. If they are open, your No.1 passes to No.3 or No.5 at the lo-post, as the main target for a shot at the basket. If they are not open, No.1 passes out to No.2, who holds the ball to set up a set play. After passing the ball, No.1 moves quickly under the basket, and around No.3, who blocks for them as they go by, to the right wing.

Sideline Screen and Move

Motion No.1 (No.49)

This is a great sideline "out of bounds" play when you are down near your offensive basket. It will probably work best when the defense is man to man, and your team is under a lot of pressure. Your No.3 takes the ball out on the sideline. I would suspect yelling "BREAK" on this play might also help in confusing the defense even more. And having them all break at once, would really confuse the defense because your players know where they are going, but the defenders do not. Your No.5 takes one step into the lane to screen for your No.4. Your No.4 zigzag zags around No.5's screen, and goes to the corner on the right wing side. After No.4 clears their screen, No.5 reverses and

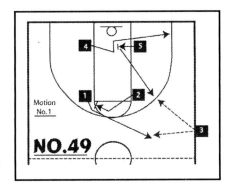

moves out to the 3 point line. Your No.2 moves toward the left elbow of the free throw line, then screens for your No.1. Your No.1 goes around the screen, and moves directly and quickly to the right side high wing area. All of this has to take place very quickly to make sure your No.1 is free to get the pass from No.3 on the sideline. To further confuse the defense, your No.3 out on the sideline wants to look towards No.4 as if they want to pass to them, but all the time knowing they are going to pass to No.1 And if for some reason your No.1 is covered, your No.5 would be the next choice to receive the pass.

Motion No.2 (No.50)

       You would use motion No.2 if you need to score quick, and want the play progression to go immediately to the basket, instead of taking time to set up and position for a set play when no one is open off motion No.1. The problem is going to be if all of this takes

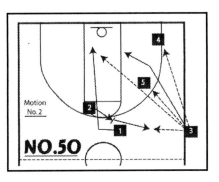

too much time, you are going to get a penalty for taking longer than 5 seconds (rule for most youth teams) to get the ball in. So if you see the play is going to take more than 5 seconds, then you will probably have to take a time out. You are going to have to explain to your players that they will have to count by 1000's, to make sure they don't run out of time.

For teams that want to run the motion No.2 progression, here is how it works. Your No.2 screens again for your No.1, just as they get into position. Then here is where it gets real tricky. There are 4 options from this point.

Option 1: No.1 reverses and cuts (flashes) to the basket, for a lob throw from your No. 3.

Option 2: Your No.3 passes to your No.5, who passes to No.1 for a shot.

Option 3: Your No.5 hands off to your No.3 as they go by, and cut and drive to the basket.

Option 4: Your No.3 passes to your No.4 out on the right wing. No.4 looks for your No.1, 3, or 5, to pass to. They take the shot. If nothing is open for No.4, then reload the offense for another play.

It's a legitimate play that some teams use (high school or college maybe), but I think it's going to be to complex, and maybe hard to remember for the little kids. If you learn to work the motion No.1 option real well, then you will probably never need to go to motion No.2, to in bound the ball within the 5 seconds.

Sideline "Double 2"

This is another out of bounds play that has to be run very fast, to not violate the 5 second rule. I'm not sure the real little kids can run motion 1 or 2 on this play either. It's something you will have to try, and time it.

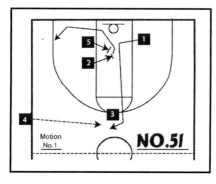

Motion No.1 (No.51)

This is a nice little play for "out of bounds" that will confuse the defense, especially the little kids. It's a 2 part motion play, but you should be able to inbound the ball before the 5 seconds are up. First your No. 4 takes the ball out on the sideline. Your No.2 and No.5 fake a double screen for your No.1 player. No.1 then cuts and flashes out to the point at the top of the key, using

No.3 as a block so they can either get the pass or shoot. Your No. 2 breaks off the screen, cuts, and curls around your No.5 towards the 3 point circle on the left wing. No.4 passes the ball to your No.1, who looks to pass, or shoot if they are clear.

Motion No.2 (No.52)
When your No.1 gets the ball they dribble over to the right wing area, to get a better angle for the continuation of the play. Then your No.4 and No.5 players do a double screen on the defender so that your No.2 can get through around them, out to the top of the left wing

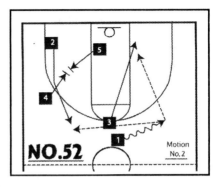

area. Your No.3 player cuts to the right side lo-post area, to block or to screen. No.1 then looks to pass to either No.3 or No.2 if they are open for a shot. This play can work even if the defense is playing "man to man" because the double screens and the fakes free up players to get the inbounds pass, or make shots.

Breaking the Press Offensive Plays

As you know, the rules will not let the little kids work the press, except in certain situations at the end of the game, and in the lower age groups. When they get older, teach them how beating the press works so that when it is used, they know how to break it.

Sideline Press Breaker

Motion No.1 (No.53)
Your No.5 takes the ball out at the sideline. Your No.5 yells "BREAK" then your No.1 screens for your No.2, who breaks for the basket. If No.2 gets open, your No.5 passes them the ball. They either dribble it in for a lay up, or they stop and shoot a short jump shot. No.4 stays back at the other end of the court as a safety, in case there is a steal or a turnover.

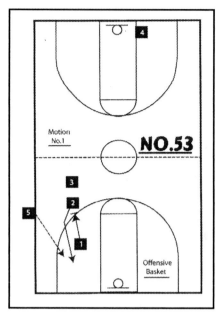

Motion No.2 (No.54)

There are several options here. When your No.1 can see that the pass is not going to No.2, they gets a screen from your No.3 player, reverse their direction, go around, and break for the basket. The play then goes 2 on 1 to the basket. The problem with this play is going to be the 5 second rule. Your players will have to count by 1000's and move quickly so that your No.5 can inbound the ball in time.

Motion No.3 (No.55)

If your No.1 can see that there is no room to break for the basket, they go around the No.3 screen, and out towards the center court. Your No.5 then passes them the ball, and they reload the offense. And remember, the pass has to get out to your No.1 before the time runs out. If time is running short as they count, No. 1 has to get the pass as they run by No.5. Your No.2 breaks for the right wing area to decoy defenders into following them, and clearing the area around the basket.

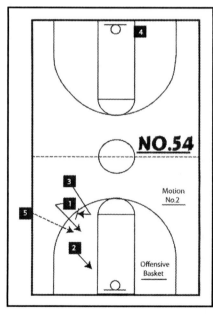

Full Court Press Breakers

Some simple rules, and strategy, for beating the full court press. **Stay calm**, think what you are doing. **Attack**, be positive and attack the pressure. *Use 3 Looks*, look up the court and not down at the ball, look before you pass, look before you dribble, don't dribble unless you have to, sharp quick passes beat the press not dribbling. *Avoid trap areas* (see the diagram), keep away from these areas. *Getting the ball inbounds*, inbound the ball quickly before the defense can set up. *Quick accurate passing*, find the open man and make quick accurate passes. *Receivers meet the pass*, go to the ball and get open. *Use*

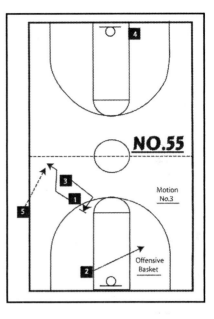

the whole court, reverse the ball to the opposite side if you have to. *Have a standard press break play*, one that works for you, then yell "PRESS BREAK" to them when you see it coming.

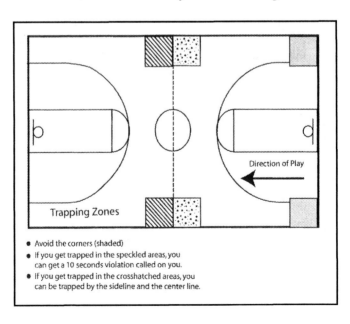

- Avoid the corners (shaded)
- If you get trapped in the speckled areas, you can get a 10 seconds violation called on you.
- If you get trapped in the crosshatched areas, you can be trapped by the sideline and the center line.

39

Beating the 1-2-1-1 Full Court Press

    The weakness of the 1-2-1-1 is up the sideline, or at mid court. Have one of your post players (No. 4 or No.5) inbound the ball as quickly as possible. You will have to practice this so that everyone knows their positions, and goes to them quickly before the press can set up.

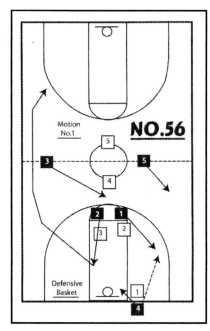

Motion No.1 (No.56)

    Your No.4 player takes the ball out at the base line. Next they yell "BREAK", and your primary target No.1 comes back down towards the ball on the right side of the court. If they are open they get the inbounds pass. Your No.2 player breaks down towards the basket in the lane, and looks for a pass if they are open and No.1 is not. If the pass goes over to No.1, then No.2 reverses and breaks back up the court on the left sideline. At the same time your No.3 player breaks to the top of the key, and No.5 breaks to the right wing area. After the pass is made, your No.4 player moves across and up the lane the lane, from under the basket.

Motion No.2 (No.57)

    Once the ball has been inbounded, and your No.1 has the ball, they quickly pass to your No.5, No.3, or No.4. With No.5 being the primary target, and next No.3, and your No.4 last as a safety. If No.5 gets the pass the rest of the team goes immediately into a fast break set play down the court. If your No. 3 gets the pass, they immediately pass to your No.2 who has stopped over on the left sideline near center court. If your No.4 player gets the pass they immediately pass to either No.2 or No.3, with No.2 being the primary target. Once the ball is basically out of the back court, you can go into secondary fast break set play.

The 4 Across Press Breaker
    The 4 across press breaker is a little different than a "stack" type set. It is more of a spread, to make it easier to get someone open for the inbounds pass. Also it's different, and gives another confusing look to a young defensive team.

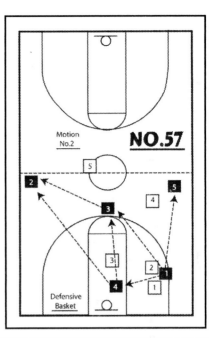

Option 1, motion 1 (No.58)
    Your No.5 player takes the ball out at the base line. They yell "BREAK", and your No.3 fakes going in towards the base line, then reverses and breaks back up the right sideline. At the same time your No.2, and No.4 players, run a double screen for your No.1 player. Your No.1 then starts back

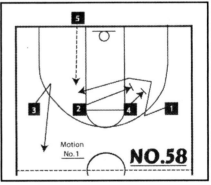

out toward the top of the key, runs their defender into the screen, then reverses and cuts back toward the base line, around the screen, and over to the right side of the lane looking for the inbounds pass.

Option 1, motion 2 (No.59)
    When your No.1 gets the ball, they start to dribble up the court, then look to quickly pass to your No.3 or No.4. After making the inbounds pass, your No.5 moves into the lane and goes up the middle of the court. Whoever gets the pass can then go into a

41

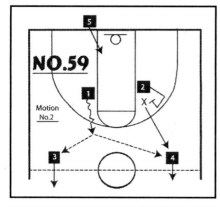

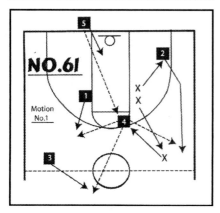

secondary fast break set play up the court. Your No.2 back screens or blocks the backside.

Option 2, motion 1 (No.60)

If your No.1 player is covered, the second option is for No.5 to inbounds pass to your No.2 player in the corner. They immediately pass to either your No.1 or No.4, whoever is open. No.1 is the primary receiver, and No.4 the secondary receiver. Whoever gets the pass can then go into a secondary fast break set play up the court. No.5 is the "trailer" on the fast break.

Option 3, motion 1 (No.61)

Your No.4 player has to watch and see if the pass does not go to your No.1 or No.2, in which case they stop and go back to the top of the key for the inbounds pass as a safety valve. When they get the pass they immediately pass to either No.1 or No.2 cutting up court. With No.1 being the prime target. If either one of them is not open, No.4 makes a long pass to No.3 cutting to the middle of the court. Whoever gets the pass can then go into a secondary fast break set play up the court. No.5 is the "trailer" on the fast break.

42

Option 4, Four Fly (No.62)

This is a special option play, for when there is only a few seconds left on the clock. Your No.5 player quickly takes the ball out at the base line. They yell "BREAK", and your No.2 and No.4 still do the double screen.

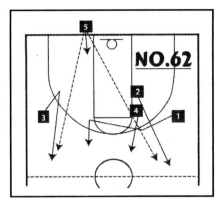

Except this time your No.1 cuts over the top of the double screen to the right side lane elbow. As soon as No.1 rubs across the shoulder of your No.4, your No.2 takes off on the fly up the court along the left side of the court lane, for a long pass from your No.5 at the base line. No.3 comes in a few steps on a fake, then reverses and flies down the court on the right side. If No.2 is covered, No.5 passes to No.3 on a fly pattern down the right side of the court lane. No.4 comes off the screen, and cuts down the middle of the court. When No.1 gets to the lane elbow, they turn and fly down the court in the middle. If they get the ball and get jammed or stopped, No.2 can pass to No.3, flying down the court across from them.

Simplified 4 Across Press Breaker

This is a little different player positioning that I think makes it a little easier for the little kids to understand. A little less movement, and quicker too.

Motion No.1 (No.63)

Your No.5 player takes the ball out at the base line. Your No.1 and No.2 line up on the inside on this one. No.5 yells "BREAK", and instead of a double screen,

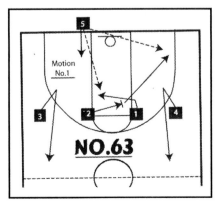

your No.2 sets a screen for your No.1. Your No.1 then moves around in back of the screen, and gets the inbounds pass from No.5. At the same time your No.3 and No.4 players both fake a move towards No.5, like they are going to get the pass, then both turn around and break back up court in the sideline lanes. Your No.2 moves to the left side corner after screening, to act as a safety valve for the inbounds pass.

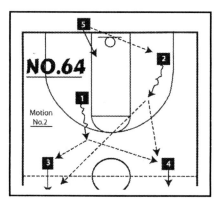

NO.64

Motion
No.2

Motion No.2 (No.64)
Your No.1 gets the inbounds pass, dribbles a few feet up court, then looks to pass to either your No.3 or No.4 players cutting down the court. If the defenders collapse on your No.1, then No.5 passes to your No.2 in the corner. Then they start to dribble up the court, and look for your No.3 or No.4 players to pass to. Whoever gets the pass can then go into a secondary fast break set play up the court. No.5 is the "trailer" on the fast break.

Delay Offensive Plays

Sometimes you need a delay play when you need to take time off the clock, like maybe near the end of the game when you are ahead in the score. Here is a good play to use. Also if you have the lead and the opponent changes to a zone defense, the counter strategy is go to the spread, make them go into a man to man and come out at you. However if the defenders do come way out after you, and your No.1 (your key player in the middle) or any of the other players can see an uncontested easy lay up, tell them to take it. Coaches sometimes call these plays "butter with a spread", or just "butter", or "soft butter".

The 4 Corners Spread ("Butter with a Spread")
The way it is set up, there are some "RULES" for each of your players to follow:

Chaser Point Guard (your No.1) **No.65**

1. When dribbling, pass before a double team collapses on you.
2. After passing, cut and quickly get open to receive the pass back to you.
3. If you can't get the pass back, cut to the basket, or replace either No.2 or No.3 in the corner.

Wing Players (your No.2 and No.3 players) **No.65**

1. Make sure you stay in the corners, about 6 feet from half court line and the sideline.
2. If not pressured after receiving a pass, hold the ball until the defense comes out to you, then pass the ball back to No.1.

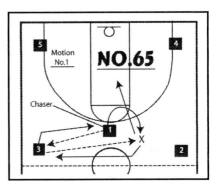

3. If the defense is blocking No.1 from getting the pass back, dribble the ball to center court and become the new chaser (No.1). The old chaser moves to the vacated corner where NO. 3 was.

Post Players (No.4 and No.5)

1. If the pass goes to the opposite corner, the weak side player cuts to the low post on the ball side, for a block or screen **(No.66)**.
2. If the post players defender moves over to trap the chaser (No.1), then quickly cut to the basket for a pass from No.1. Then go for the lay up **(No.67)**.

45

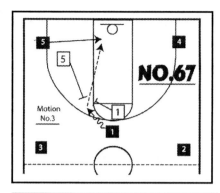

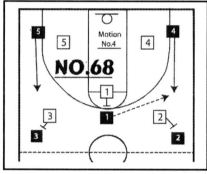

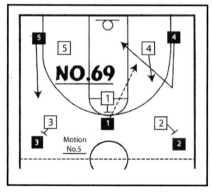

3. If the chaser or a wing player is in trouble, or they stop their dribble, cut up the sideline to a spot in line with the free throw line extended, and look to receive a pass **(No.68)**.

4. If the post player guarding them over plays them, and keeps them from receiving the pass, then they cut back quickly to the basket for a pass from No.1 **(No.69)**.

Some Additional Delay Strategy

Going for the Last Shot of a Quarter ("Butter")

What you try to do is run the clock down to the last 10-15 seconds. Then the coach yells "GO". All the corners then move in towards the basket, and everyone works together to get a good shot off. Whoever has the ball tries to make a shot. If the shot *is not* open, they look to pass to whoever looks most open, and they take the shot.

Even if they miss there may be time for a rebound, and a second shot opportunity if your players crash the board. By then there is probably not enough time for the opposition to make a play if you do turn it over. Maybe only 4 or 5 seconds are left, and your players should be able to play good defense for that long. Make sure though that your players are in position in the "4 corners", with a minute or 40 seconds to go on the clock.

5 or 6 Minutes left in the Game ("Soft Butter")

The situation is, there is 4 or 5 minutes left in the game and you are up maybe 6 or 8 points. What you *don't* want to do is, go into a full delay, and quit continuing to score. What you *do* want to do is be patient and run some time off the clock. So what you do is go into a 4 corners ("Soft Butter") offense, take your time and look for quality high percentage shots, or fouls, and a chance to go to the free throw line. Sometimes the defense thinks you are going into a full delay, but when they least expect it, you attack the basket for a lay up.

This is also a good strategy to use when you have the lead, and the defense is sitting back in a 2-3 zone preventing your team from having an inside game, and your guards from penetrating. The "4 corners" offense forces the defense to come out of their zone and play man to man. This opens up the middle for your inside game. The only problem is going to be if you are dealing with a shot clock, then you can only use this offense for a short period of time.

Tip Off Offensive Plays

The "tip off" is not a big deal like it used to be, when "jumped balls" were actually jumped. However if you have a tall center that is a good jumper, here is a play you can use. It's probably better to get possession when you can if possible. So go for it.

Tip Quick Out Crash

Motion No.1 (No.70)

Your players basically line up in a 1-3-1 set at center

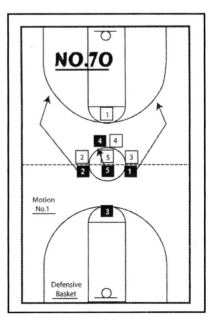

court. Have your taller players practice to see who is the best "tipper" on jump balls. That player will be your No.5. It may be your center, or even a forward that is tall and a good jumper. Your No. 5 makes the tip to your No.4 player. Your No.1 and No.2 players break and cut down the sidelines. Your No.3 player stays back at the top of the key as a safety valve, in case your team loses the tip off.

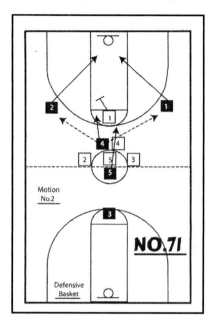

Motion No.2 (No.71)

Your No.4 player takes the tip ball, turns and immediately passes, or tip directs the ball to your No.1 or No.2 players. Whoever get the ball sprints, on a 2 on 1, to the basket for a lay up. If defender No.1 commits to either your No.1 or No.2 players, and blocks their path to the basket, they pass the ball over to the other player for the lay up. Your No.4 and No.5 players are "trailers" on the play.

If you determine you do not have a good chance for getting the ball on the tip off, you may want to just set up around the circle in a defensive line up. This may prevent your opponents from getting an easy lay up off the tip.

Defensive Plays

There are half court defensive plays, full court defensive plays, out of bounds defensive plays, fast break defensive plays, delay defensive plays, and tip off defensive plays. We will show some good "man to man" pressure defenses, and zone defenses.

Half Court Defensive Plays

Man to Man Pressure

Some general "RULES" to follow are:

48

1. Teach your players to force the ball to the sideline, and then down to the base line when at all possible. Do not allow penetration along the base line. Try to trap at the base line corner.
2. Keep defensive pressure on the ball at all times. Don't let your players back way off and let the opponent move around. Get close but don't foul.
3. Have your players let the opponents point guard pass out to the wings, but don't let them pass back to the point guard in the middle.
4. Have your players deny dribble penetration along the base line. Tell them to take a charging foul if necessary. If the defender on the dribbler gets beaten, your lo-post defender, who is fronting the opponents lo-post, has to immediately rotate to the base line to stop the dribbler.
5. Make it difficult for the opponents outside shooters to get a shot off. Have your players get their hands up in front of them.
6. Tell your players not to reach in. Unless they are really good at it, they will probably get the foul called on them. And as you reach in you are off balance, and that might let the opponent hook you and go around. If they do reach in, tell them to reach in on the inside (middle of the court side) of the opponent, forcing them to go more to the outside of the court, away from the basket.
7. Teach your players to use "help and recover" techniques. This means your team mates come over to "help" your player if they do get beaten by the opponent. This gives them time to "recover" and get back to their man.

Defensive Positioning off the Ball

Position No.1 (No.72)
    Many teams come down and go into a 2 in, 3 out

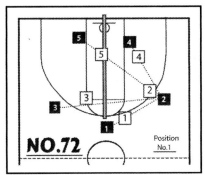

offense. First tell your players to pretend there is an imaginary line up the middle of the court, called the "help side line" (shown as the heavy line splitting the basket). Then also have them imagine an imaginary line drawn from the ball to each offensive player (shown as a dotted line). Then each player locates, called one pass away, in a "deny" mode, and stays on the dotted line.

Your No.4 and No.5 players take the lo-post opponents. Your No.2 stays right on the opponents No.2. Your No.1. stays right on the opponents No.1. Your No.3 player locates at the weak side free throw line elbow. No.3 will let the pass go to their No.3 out on the wing, but as soon as their No.3 gets the pass they go out and get right on them so that they can not pass the ball back over to their No.1 at the top of the key. If you decide you want to deny the pass to their No.3 out on the wing, you have your No.3 move over on the dotted line and front them.

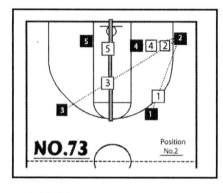

Position No.2 (No.73)

The defenders (your No.3 and No.5 players), located as two passes away, are called "help side" players. When the ball gets down in the corner, they are located with one foot on the "help side" line. It helps them prevent inside passing, and dribble penetration. Tell them to use their peripheral vision, to always keep sight of the ball and their man. Some coaches call this the "pistol" positions. You can illustrate this to them by having them use both of their index fingers pointed as if shooting a gun. First one finger at the ball, then the other finger pointed at the man, with both arms out stretched. Another term coaches will use for this is, the "ball-you-man" positioning. Your No.1, 2, and 4, players slide over and front their man opponents, staying on the dotted line.

Position No.3 (No.74)

Your No.5 is now in a good position to deny the backside lob over pass to their No.5 at the lo- post, or dribble penetration by their No.2. No.4 blocks No.2. Take notice (from play No.72 and

73) of how your No.5 and No.3 rotate when the ball moves to the corner. Also take notice that whenever the ball is below the free throw line, the "help side" defenders (your No.3 and No.5) have one foot on the help side line.

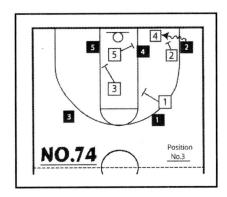

Position No.4 (No.75)

When a bounce pass or a lob throw goes over to the offensive No.3 player out on the wing, notice how the defense shifts and rotates over. Your No.1, 3, and 5, players stay on the dotted line. Your No.4 and No.1 are on the center "help side line". Your No.2 is kind of splitting the distance between their No.2 offensive man, and along the edge of the lane.

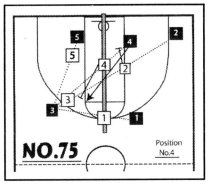

If offensive player No.4 makes a move up to the left side free throw line elbow, your No.4 moves right up along with them. What they try to do is get one hand in front of them to "deny" them the pass from offensive player No. 3 on the wing. Your No.2 player has to be ready to move towards offensive player No.4 in case a lob pass goes over to them from offensive player No.3.

Position No.5 (No.76)

To help make it harder for the offensive players to beat your players guarding them, with a dribble penetration, have them get a few steps closer to the ball than the one pass away

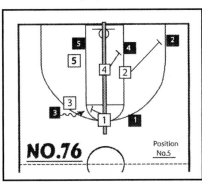

distance. Do this when the opposition has a very good penetrating guard. Also remember that if the opposition has a very good long distance, or 3 point shooter located out on one of the wing areas, it may be better to have your player guarding them go back in a "deny" position, and not leave them to give help. Normally when the offensive No.3 player tries to dribble penetrate, your No.1 player has to come over and give help.

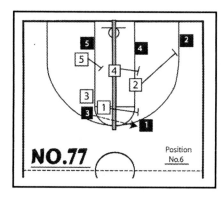

NO.77

Position No.6

Position No.6 (No.77)

This play as well as No.76 show how to give help and recover on the perimeter areas. When offensive player No.3 is denied dribble penetration, they have to pass the ball out to their No.1 player. Your defender player No.1 has to move out quickly to the on ball "deny" position.

Your No.3 player stays in the "deny" position while your No.2 and No.4 players move quickly to their "deny positions. Your No.5 player moves to their "help side" position. In teaching "help and recover", tell your players to move their feet quickly to establish position, and prevent the dribble move. What they *don't* want to do is reach in.

Defending Post Players

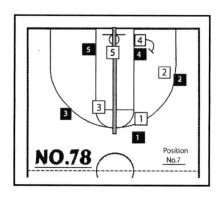

NO.78

Position No.7

Position No.7 (No.78)

Coaches say make every effort to keep the ball out of the low post. Two things usually happen (both bad) when the offense gets the ball into the lo-post, the first is they score, and second is a defender commits a foul. Most coaches say 1/2 to 3/4 front the offensive lo-post player

52

(No.4) from the base line side, if they are taller. That is keeping one foot between the player and the basket, and one hand as a bar in front of them. If they are shorter though, a full front position is advised. Teach your lo-post defensive players to work on their good footwork. They will have to be quick and agile to "deny" offensive lo-post players.

Position No.8 (No. 79)

When the offensive player No.2 can't get the ball into their No.4, they will pass back to their No.1. As soon as your No.4 player can see the ball go over to offensive player No.1 out at the point, they move around to the inside and 1/2 to 3/4 front offensive player No.4. They also keep both feet to the side, and use one arm in front to bar the pass.

NO.79　　　Position No.8

Position No.9 (No.80)

What your player No.4 wants to do is hold their 1/2 to 3/4 front position on offensive player No.4 (shown in dotted). What they *don't* want to do is go all the way around front on the top (shown in solid) because this will let No.4 get the ball and hook them on the inside, to go to the basket.

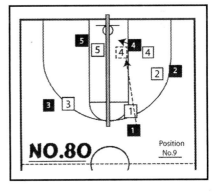

NO.80　　　Position No.9

Position No.10 (No.81)

When the pass goes from offensive player No.1 out to No.2 on the wing, your

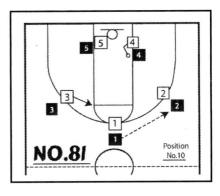

NO.81　　　Position No.10

No.3 player slides over to the left elbow of the free throw line. Your No.4 player slides over just far enough to "deny" offensive No.4 player to pin or hook them as they try take the inside path to the basket. If your No.4 tries to front offensive player No.4, they could get the pass and have an easy spin to the basket (see position No.9).

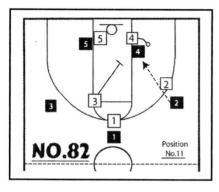

NO.82

Position No.11

Position No.11 (No.82)

When a pass does go in to offensive No.4, your No.4 holds their position No.10) and still "denies" No.4 the base line. Your No.3 player quickly comes down to help, "denying" offensive No.4 the inside move to the basket. Offensive No.4 will then probably have to kick the ball back out to their No.1 or No.2. This should keep the opponents lo-post from making an easy basket.

Defending Cutters

Most defensive minded coaches say, you should always "deny" a pass to a cutter moving through the lane. Basically all defenders need to stay between their man and the ball.

One technique some defenders use is to "bump the cutter" off of their intended pathway. They do this by getting position on the cutter, then riding them away from the basket. This is a special skill you will have to work on, by practicing with them. Teach them to beat the cutter to a certain spot on the floor, by observing as they move, to where they think the cutter is going. Both players are entitled to that certain spot on the floor, it just depends on who gets there first. Teach them this kind of thinking. Many times you can get "charging" called.

General cuts to defend are, cuts from the weak side wing (with or without screens), "give and go's", flash cuts to either hi or lo-post, and back-cuts. Teach your players to recognize them.

Position No.12 (No.83)

A special cut sometimes used is the "curl-cut". Defending against this offensive play (not to common) is going to take a fast, and smart player. First they will have to recognize it, then second follow it. The offensive player No.2 makes a cut to the basket. Your

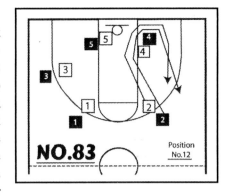

No.2 has to "chase" them all the way around offensive No.4, and back out to the 3 point circle.

Position No.13 (No.84)

What can happen is, if your No.2 gives up the "chase" and waits to pick them up when they come back around, offensive No.2 goes to the corner and is clear for a 3 point shot. Then offensive player No.1 lobs a long pass over to them for the shot.

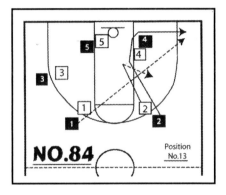

Defending Against Screens

Most defensive minded coaches say, you must have a plan against "screens". If you don't, a good team will see that and make your players really look bad. As you can probably see by now is, screens are a big part of the offensive play book. Inside screens should be switched between your No.4 and No.5 players because you probably won't have a size, or quickness, mismatch. On outside perimeter screens, you will have to decide, depending on the team you are playing, whether you want to "switch", "fight through them", or "slide" under them. Switching on perimeter screens can lead to a size or quickness mismatch match. This is especially true when a big post player steps outside to set a screen for a guard.

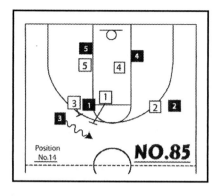

On-Ball Screens

Position No.14 (No.85)

The opponents No.2 player has the ball. It's a case when you can probably fight over the screen rather than "switching". Your No.1 comes over and fakes a switch by stepping out against offensive player No.3. What this does is "deny" No.3 to go up the lane, and forces them to go outside. That lets your No.3 to fight over the top of the screen, and stay on the opponent. Your No.1 must quickly go back to covering their man. Again this is another example of "help and recover". These are also plays that you have to teach your players to communicate with each other on.

Off-Ball Screen

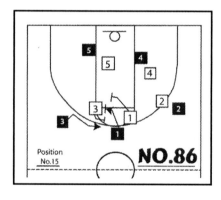

Position No.15 (No.86)

Offensive player No.2 has the ball. In this play your No.3 has dropped down to the left side of the free throw line at "help side". Offensive player No.3 starts to move over and break for a drive down the lane.

Offensive player No.1 comes right at your No.3 for a screen or block. What your No.1 player has to do is move over to help. This forces offensive player No.3 go out wider at the top of the key. And this leaves more room for your No.3 to fight over the top of the screen, and stay with offensive player No.3 as they move across. Your No.1 has to then slide back over and stay with their No.1.

56

Position No. 16 (No.87)

One of the other alternatives is, your No.3 player rolls off the screen and slides under and around the screener, to stay with offensive player No.3. Then your No.1 stays with their No.1.

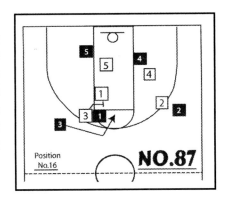

Position No. 17 (No.88)

The other alternative is to "switch", where your No.1 stays with their No.3, and your No.3 stays with their No.1. The problem is during the "switch", your No.3 has to step under and be careful not to get sealed off on the outside, letting their No.1 to roll off on the inside and down towards the basket.

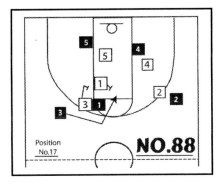

Inside Post Screen

Position No. 18 (No.89)

When the opponents No.2 player has the ball on the wing, most coaches say it is better to "switch" inside post screens. Here is the rule your post players follow. Your player fronting their lo-post player always takes the low cutter while your other lo-post defender always takes the high cutter.

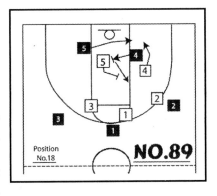

The opponents No.2 player has the ball. Offensive player No.5 cuts low. Offensive player No.4 screens your No.5 player

57

away from the cutter. Your No.4 switches and continues to front offensive player No.5 as they come around. Your No.5 player "switches" and follows No.4, after they screen, as they break towards the right side of the lane.

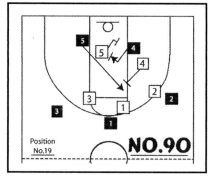

Position No. 19 (No.90)
Offensive player No.5 cuts high (most common move) to the right side of the lane. Your No.4 "switches" and moves down the lane to cover No.5, and deny them the pass from No.2. Offensive player No.4 screens your player No.5, who drops low to cover offensive player No.4 on the "switch".

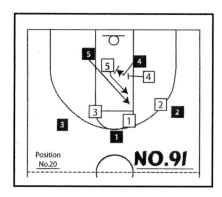

Position No.20 (No.91)
Sometimes the "switch" is not necessary. When offensive player No.5 cuts high, your No.5 moves up the lane and over the top of the screen, to cover them from the pass from offensive player No.2. Your player No.4 just slides over, and continues to front offensive player No.4 as they attempt to screen No.5.

Down screens

Position No.21 (No.92)
The opponents No.1 has the ball. On the "switch", offensive player No.2 pretends to cut down into the lane for a pass, but then screens and blocks your No.4 . Your No.2 player chases offensive No.2 into the lane. When the screener stops your No.2 is in a good position to "switch", and pick up the cutter, offensive player No.4, coming around the screen.

Position No.22 (No.93)

There can be a problem though. This is what could happen if the "switch" is made. The first problem is there could be a big-little mismatch match when your No.2 starts to cover offensive player No.4. The second problem can happen if offensive player No.4 reads the "switch", turns, and cuts out to the right wing for a pass from offensive player No.1. In that case your No. 2 player could easily get trapped and caught inside. This leaves offensive player No.4 open, out on the perimeter, for a jumper or a 3 point shot.

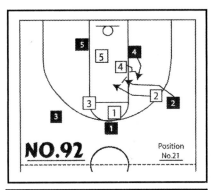

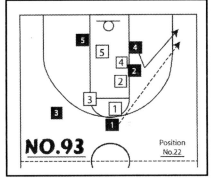

Back screens

Position No.23 (No. 94)

The opponents No.1 has the ball. This is a so called "back-door" cut to the basket. The offensive player No.2 cuts around offensive player No.4, and heads for the basket. Offensive player No. 4 moves out towards the perimeter and screens your player No.2. Your player No.4 will "switch", and cover offensive player No.2 from getting a pass on the inside.

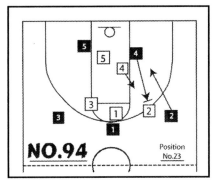

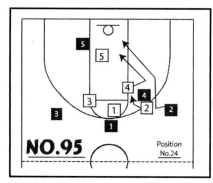

Position No.24 (No. 95)

Most good defensive coaches say make this "switch" instead. Your player No.4 has to recognize the back-door play, and call out to your No.2 player that the back screen is coming. What your No.2 has to do then is, step in front of and around No.4 to get inside positioning. This is to keep them from getting caught on the outside of the screen. There is one problem with this play, you may end up with a big-little mismatch match with your No.2 player and offensive player No.4.

So the first chance they get, your No.2 and No.4 want to "switch" back to the players they were guarding. If the ball goes over to the weak side, then that is a good time to make the "switch" back. Meanwhile your No.4 player, recognizing the back screen, steps over, picks up offensive player cutting to the basket and stays right with them. This prevents offensive No.1 from making a pass or lob throw to them for the lay up, or jumper.

Out of Bounds Defenses

Many coaches like to play the base line out of bounds, with a 2-3 zone. Here is a good man-to-man pressure defense to especially keep from getting burned inside.

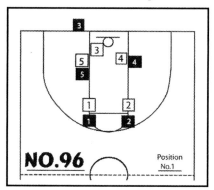

Man-to-Man Box
Position No.1 (No.96)

This is called the "box out of bounds" play. If you look at it, is really just the "box and 1" turned around at the base line. The exception is your No.3 plays a one man zone to "deny" passes inside around the basket. The rest of your players form a box and guard the lane for any inside short passes to the offensive inside players.

Position No.2 (No.97)
Now here is where it changes. Offensive player No.3 passes the ball out to offensive player No.1, who breaks out into the left wing area to get the pass.
As soon as the inbounds pass is made,

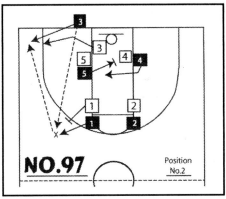

and offensive player No.3 breaks for the left corner, your No.3 player breaks and moves out to cover No.3, using a man-to-man defense to cover them. As soon as offensive player No.1 gets the ball they will pass it out to No.3 in the corner. Offensive player No.5 attempts to screen your player No.4. Offensive player No.4 breaks into the lane for a possible inside pass.

Position No.3 (No.98)
Your No.4 and No.5 post players "switch" on the screen. Your player No.4 "switches", and steps around and under No.5's screen, to get inside positioning. Your No.5 "switches", and picks up offensive No.4 breaking

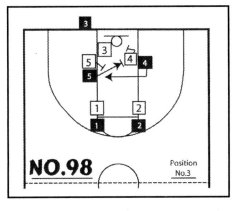

into the lane. Offensive No.1 and No.2 will probably stay out on the perimeter through all this, as a safety to get the inbounds pass. Just let them get the ball if they are open way out on the perimeter. They are usually the shooters with little kids teams, and it's harder for them to make the long outside shots. Then reload and go into your regular defense, zone or whatever.

61

Man-to-Man Stack

This is a tough offensive "out of bounds" play to defense, especially for the little kids. There are so many different ways to offensively load this positioning. Players can go different ways, and they can be put in different locations within the stack. We will not try to show every possibility, but we will show a number of ways the opponents will try to trick you and get open. If you can break right with them, protect the basket inside, and keep them from making the inbounds pass for too long of time (5 seconds), they may make a mistake and make a bad pass you can intercept for a steal. The idea with the man-to-man defense is stay right with them as close as you can without fouling them.

Position No.1 (No.99)

I like the 3 in 2 out basic defense against the "stack". Usually the offense has 2 or 3 plays off the stack. The offensive

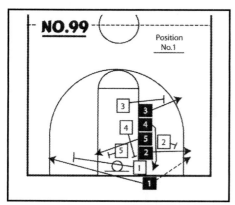

out of bounds ball holder will hold up 1, 2, or 3, fingers as to which play they want to run. They will yell "BREAK", and the players all move. What you want your players to do is break with them if possible. In this particular play, offensive player No.2 breaks for the left wing corner, to get a quick inbounds pass from No.1.

After throwing in the ball, their No.1 breaks for the right wing corner, to open up the left lo-post area. Your No.1 follows. Their No.5 breaks the opposite way to the right lo-post. Your No.5 has to slide over with them, but stay on the "help line". Your No.2 moves out to stay on their No.2. Their No.4 then tries to cut down to the left lo-post. Your No.4 has to move down with them so that they will not get open at the left lo-post. Their No.3 cuts to the left wing perimeter, to be open for a safety valve inbounds pass. Your No.3 has to stay right with them.

Position No.2 (No.100)

Sometimes the defense will send their No.3 out of bounds to make the pass. This is to free up guards No.1 and No.2 to get the inbounds pass. Both of them break to the left wing 3 point circle. Your No.1 and No.2 players have to break with them, and stay close. Their No.4 player will break to the right side of the lane, hoping to pull your No.4 with them, to free up some space. Your No.4 has to slide across, but stay on the "help line". Their No.5 player cuts straight down to the left lo-post. Your No.5 drops down to cover, but also

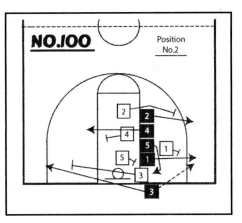

stays on the "help line". Their No.3 inbounds the ball to their No.1 as soon as they break, and get clear. Your No.1 closes on them, then and stays right with them, denying them the inside route to the basket. After their No.3 makes the inbounds pass, they cut to the right side corner. Your No.3 has to move out with them, so they are not wide open for a long 3 point shot.

Position No.3 (No.101)

Sometimes teams will stack up on the right side edge of the lane, instead of the left side. This is to confuse your defense. It's still the same sideways break of some kind though. And if you notice, it's still basically your center and the 2 forwards (3 in) around the lane, and your 2 guards (2 out) are on the perimeter.

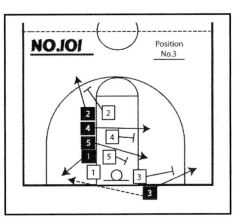

63

It's just where they locate each time is going to depend on where their counterpart offensive players are within the stack. You have to teach your players to recognize what is happening, and then cover their counterpart players. Also teach them to communicate to each other what is happening.

Their No.3 inbounds to their No.1, then cuts to the left wing corner. Your No.3 follows. Your No.1 moves right out to cover their No.1. Their No.2 breaks for the top of the right wing area. Your No.2 follows. Their No.4 and No.5 players both break towards the left wing side, hoping to pull your No. 4 and No.5 with them. This is to free up open space around the basket, for their No.1 to try and drive the lane and score. Your players move out to the edge, but keep one foot on the "help line".

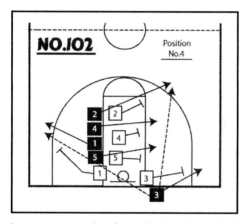

Position   No. 4 (No. 102)

Here again, their No.3 takes the ball out of bounds, to try and get the ball to their quicker guards (No.1 and No.2). Notice how they move their No.1 up in the stack so that they can get free out on the wing. This is what you have to recognize from the bench, and your players out on the court. The offense will usually only have a few plays, you have to figure out from the bench where they are putting their players in the stack, then communicate that to your players on the court.

Their No.3 inbounds to their No.1 out on the wing, then cuts to the left wing corner. Your No.3 follows. Your No.1 has to be ready to move right out to cover their No.1 as soon as they notice No.1 higher up in the stack. The "CLUE" is, that's why they are higher up in the stack, so they can get clear on the wing for the inbounds pass. Their No.4 and No.5 players both break towards the left wing side, hoping to pull your No. 4 and No.5 with them out on the wing. Again, this is to free up open space around the basket, for their No.1 to drive the lane, or try a short jump shot. Their No.2

breaks for the top left wing area as a safety valve, in case No.1 is covered, for the inbounds pass. Your No.2 follows.

Zone Defenses

The 1-3-1 Zone Trap

This is a very common half court defense. To understand how this works, you will have to explain to your players about how the court is divided up into the zones. The half court is divided up, above and below the free throw line, and down the middle with a left side and a right side.

Here are your player "RULES":

For your Point (1), Middle (4), Bottom (5) players (No.103)

For all 3 players, the court is divided into above the free throw line, and below the free throw line. Special "RULES" for your No.1 (point) player are:

1. When the ball is above the free throw line they play right on the ball.
2. When the ball is below the free throw line, your No.1 swings around and "denies" any passes out of the corner.

Special "RULES" for your No.4 (middle) player are:

1. When the ball is above the free throw line, they "deny" any pass into the hi-post area.
2. When the ball is below the free throw line, No.4 "denies" any passes into the ball side lo-post area.

Special "RULES" for your No.5 (bottom) player are:

1. When the ball is above the free throw line, your No.5 is blocking in front of the ball side opponent.
2. When the ball is below the free throw line, your No.5 is on the ball.

For your Wing Players 2 and 3 (No.103)

The court is divided down the middle with a left side and a right side. When the ball is on their side of the court, your No.2 or No.3 (wing) player is on the ball, and guarding. When the ball is above the free throw line, and on the other side of the court, your

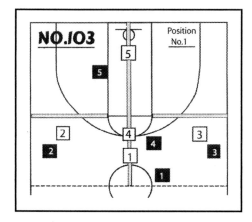

No.2 or No.3 player "denies" the cross court pass. When the ball is below the free throw line, and on the other side of the court, your No.2 or No.3 player "denies" the pass into the ball side hi-post area.

When the Ball is in the Top Corners (No.104)

When the ball is in the top right corner, your No.1 and No.3 move over to trap offensive player No.1. Players legs should be

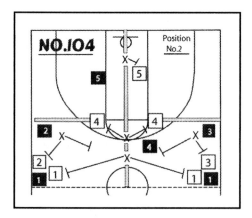

crossed and interlocked so that No.1 can't dribble the ball out. Your No.2 player moves over towards the top of the key, and "denies" any cross court passes. Your No.4 "denies" any passes into the right hi-post. Your No.5 "denies" any passes into the right lo-post.

When the ball is in the top left corner, your No.1 and No.2 move over to trap offensive player No.1. Your No.3 player moves over towards the top of the key, and "denies" any cross court passes. Your No.4 "denies" any passes into the left hi-post. Your No.5 "denies" any passes into the left lo-post.

When the Ball is in the Bottom Corners (No.105)

When the ball is in the bottom right corner, your No.3 and No.5 move over to trap offensive player No.1. Players legs should be crossed and interlocked so that No.1 can't dribble the ball out.

Your No.1 player moves over towards the right wing, and "denies" any passes back out from No.1 into the right wing area. Your No.2 "denies" any passes into the right hi-post. Your No.4 moves down and "denies" any passes into the right lo-post.

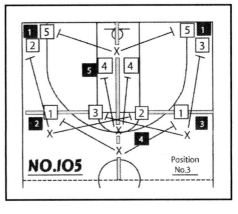

When the ball is in the bottom left corner, your No.2 and No.5 move over to trap offensive player No.1. Your No.1 player moves over towards the left wing area, and "denies" any passes back out from No.1 into the left wing area. Your No.3 "denies" any passes into the left hi-post. Your No.4 moves down and "denies" any passes into the left lo-post.

When the Ball gets into the High Post (No.106)

This is how your players react if the ball does get into the hi-post. Your wing player No.3 sprints down to the weak side lo-post as soon as they see the pass start to go into offensive player No.2 at

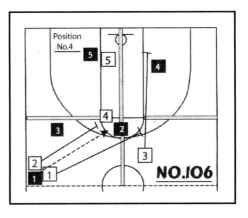

the hi-post. Your players No.1 and No.2 quickly move to the weak side hi-post area, and the strong side free throw elbow. Your No.4 player reacts, and stops offensive player No.2 from dribbling into the lane. If you notice, this has sort of formed into a 3-2 zone defense.

When the Ball gets into the Lo-Post (No.107)

Tell your players to do everything they can to keep the ball from getting into the lo-post. But if it does, this is how your players

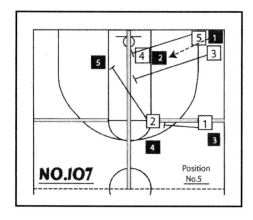

react. Offensive player No.1 is trapped and has the ball in the corner. They manage to get a pass into offensive player No.2. As soon as your player No.2 player can see the pass go in to offensive player No.2, they sprint to the weak side lo-post. Your No.4 player has to "deny" offensive player No.2 the dribble or a shot until help gets there. Your players No.3 and No.5 sprint to the low lane area for "help". Your No.1 quickly moves to the right free throw elbow, to fill the spot that was occupied by No.2.

The 2-3 (2-1-2) Zone

This defense is very good against a team with big kids, or slower kids, that like to play inside around the basket. However it can be beaten by a team that can shoot good from the outside.

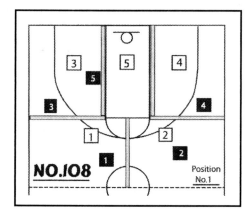

The Positioning (No.108)

The court is divided up a little differently than the 1-3-1 zone setup. Basically the court is divided into below the free throw line, and above the free throw line. Above the free throw line the court is divided down the middle, with a left half and a right half. Below the free throw line the court is divided into 3 areas (zones), the middle, the left side, and the right side.

68

When Ball is on the Wings (No.109)

When the ball goes to the left wing, the zone flip-flops and rotates, with the guards sliding over to the left. Your No.2 player has to stay right on their player No.2, to make it hard for them to dribble or pass the ball off. Notice that

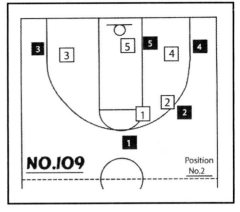

your No.1 player has moved over to the strong side free throw elbow.

Trapping the Corners (No.110)

When the ball goes to the left corner, the zone flip-flops and rotates, with a guard and a forward moving over to trap offensive player No.3 in the corner. On the right corner (shown), your players No.2 and No.4 have moved over to trap offensive player No.4. Your No.1 has slid over, taking the place of your No.2, to guard offensive player No.2 on the wing. They also have to "deny" a pass to either offensive player No.2, or No.1, trying to cut down the right side of the lane. Your No.3 has

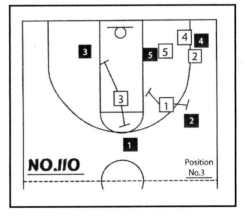

moved over to the top of the lane, below the free throw line.

They have to guard against, and "deny", any passes to either offensive player No.1, or offensive player No.3 across court at the weak side lo-post. Your No.5 has to quickly move into a lo-post blocking position to "deny" a pass in to offensive player No.5 at the strong side lo-post. If they do not get there in time, it may be an easy pass, then lay-up, or short jump shot, for offensive player No.5 to make.

69

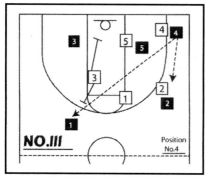

Passes from Corners out to Wings (No.111)

When the ball is in the left corner, the zone flip-flops and rotates, with a guards and a forwards moving over to the left side. On the right corner (shown), your player No.4 guards and blocks against a dribble to the basket. Your No.2 player guards and blocks offensive player No.2 from getting a pass back out into the wing area. Your No.1 player moves to the right elbow of the free throw line, to block any moves down and into the lane. Your No.3 moves back over to the middle of the lane. They have to be ready to either move quickly to the basket, or out to the perimeter, to cover or "deny" long passes. Your No.5 closely guards offensive player No.5 from getting the ball, then turning and dribbling the ball to the basket.

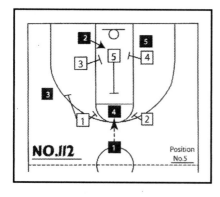

Passes into the Hi-Post (No.112)

When the pass comes into the hi-post, your No.5 player has to come up and defend the top of the key. Notice that when your No.5 comes up, this starts to look like a 2-1-2 defense. What your No.3 has to watch for is, offensive player No.2 cutting and sneaking in under the basket for a shot. In fact both your No.3 and No.4 players may have to cheat into the lane, to cover after your No.5 moves up towards the hi-post. Your No.1 covers their No.3 and No.4.

Defending the Point (No.113)

This is always a tough area to guard while in a zone defense. If you know the opponents No.2 is their best shooter, then have your No.1 defend the point area at first. Then have your No.2

sag over towards their No.2 (shown). However if their No.1 starts hitting some shots from the point, then your No.1 is going to have to come out and pressure them. This is just flip-flopped if their No.3 is their best shooter. Tell your No.1 and No.2 players to never let the opponents No.1 split between

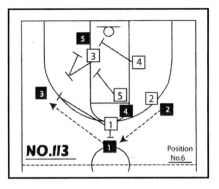

them, and dribble down the middle. You are going to have to teach both your No.1 and No.2 to work hard, and move quickly to cover both the wings and the point. Your No.3, 4, and 5, players will have to rotate as shown as the ball moves to the opposite side of the court.

On ball reversal, your No.3 player "helps" by coming out a short distance when the ball gets out to the wing on their side, then quickly drops back down to cover the lo-post. Your No.5 has to be ready to slide down to the middle of the lane to "help".

Covering Corner Skip Passes (No.114)

When the ball is in the right corner, your No.1 has to cover both the opponents No.1 or No.3 as soon as they know which player is getting the skip pass on the point or wing. If the ball is in the left corner, your No.2 has to do the covering at the point and right wing.

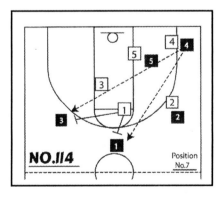

Covering Double Teamed Corner Skip Passes (No. 115)

When the ball is in the right corner, your No.3 has to cover both the corner or the wing as soon as they know which one is getting the pass. When the pass goes to the opponents No.1 at the point, your No.1 has to move out and pressure them.

71

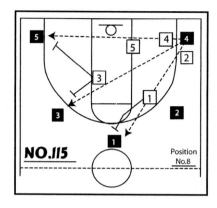

Position
No.8

Delay Defense

The 4 Corner Stopper

Coach what you are going to have to do first is, figure out why the opponent is going into a delay. If it's late in the game call a time out if possible, and let the kids know what you want them to do, so it's clear to them.

Here are some possible reasons:

1. It's a young team, a low scoring game, the opponent is ahead in the score. There is 2 minutes or so on the clock. They are afraid your team is better.
2. The opponent can't penetrate your zone defense, they want to try and force you out on the perimeter to open up inside space so they can score.
3. Both teams are good scoring teams, there is a minute or less on the clock, they are ahead by only a few points.
4. They are going for the last shot in the quarter, or the game.

After you figure out why, then you can use several strategies:

If you decide they are doing this because of reason No.1, then the best thing to do is go right out quickly and put light pressure on them, don't let them dribble around, try to make a steal, double team trap, and don't foul. Get the ball back as quick as you can. Make them take the long shots. Young kids are not so good at this.

If you decide this is because of reason No.2, then take your time, and go out and put soft pressure on them. If you are ahead, they are the team that's in the hurry. Don't help them out by rushing. Tell your players don't let them dribble around them, or cut to the basket because that's what they are going to try and do.

If you decide this is because of reason No.3, then go out and quickly put pressure on them, and try not to foul. You have to have to get the ball back so you can score. Sometimes when they see the ball go out to one of the corners, your 2 closest outside players can move in quickly and run a trap. Also with young teams the trap can sometimes cause them to get exited and make a turnover pass.

   If you decide this is because of reason No.4, then go out quickly and put pressure on them, and try not to foul. If you are ahead, take your time and play soft, but don't let them score. A trap might run down the clock if you have the players quick enough to get there and run it.

   If you are behind, and desperately need to score quickly, then you are going to have to make a steal, or trap, just to get the ball back.

Motion No.1 (No.116)

   So what you want to do is start in a 2-1-2 defensive set, then go from there. At the youth level, what the offense is probably going to use this for is stalling, that's what the 4 corners does. It usually starts with an offensive guard (No.1) dribbling in to the point. Then they just stay there until you send a player out to pressure them (No.1). The other thing their No.1 will do is, pass the ball around out to their perimeter players (No.2, 3, 4, and 5). Tell your No.2, 3, 4, and 5, perimeter players to keep looking _quickly_ back and forth, between the ball handler and the player they are guarding. They might see the pass coming and make a steal.

Motion No.2 Cutters (No.117)

   Here are 3 of the more common moves the offense makes when they need to score from this set. Their No.1 starts to dribble around your No.1 and down the edge of the lane. Your

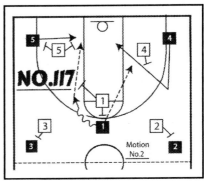

No.1 has to go out and block them. When they see your No.1 is going to block them, they will try to pass off to their No.5 cutting to the basket. Your No.5 has to recognize this play, and move to block them, or intercept the pass. If your No.1 and No.5 players don't rotate in to block, their No.1 dribbles in for a lay-up, or short jump shot. The other play they like to run is, their No.4 cuts back towards their No.2, then when they see your No.4 over commit a little, they cut back on the inside towards the lane, and get a pass from their No.1 while they drive to the basket for a lay-up. Your No.1, 4, and 5 players have to be watching for this, so they can move over to block it off.

Motion No.3 Breakers & Loopers (No.118)

Here are 3 more offensive moves to watch for. Their No.1 passes the ball over to the wing (No.3), then breaks for the basket, stops, and loops back around to the top of the key if your No.1 follows them closely. Then if their No.3 is pressured, they pass the ball back to their No.1 at the top of the key. If your No.1 does not

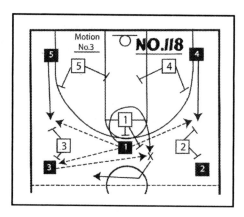

follow them, and your No.5 does not come part way over in the lane to block, No.1 cuts to the basket for a pass from their No.3, and goes for the lay-up. So you can see that you will have to work hard with your players to watch for, and counter this play.

If their wing players (No.2 and No.3) get pressured, either their No.4 or No.5 players will break back towards center court, to get a safety pass from their No.1. Teach your No.2, 3, 4, and 5, players to watch for this also, then move to cover. Another sneaky move the offense might try is, if either their No.2 or No.3 has the ball and they see their No.1 is pressured, they can "switch" and dribble the ball over to the top of the key, then they become the new No.1 while the first No.1 moves around in back, to the spot they just vacated on the wing. As you can see, defending the 4 corners can be hard work. You will have to have fast smart players to defend against the "4 corners".

Full Court Defensive Plays

1-2-2 Zone Press Defense

This is a pretty easy full court press to learn. And it's safe to run because it has back court coverage, to prevent lay-ups. There are 3 versions of this play you can use.
They are:

1. The **"80"** 3/4 court press with aggressive play, and trapping in the back court.
2. The **"70"** press with soft pressure , designed to control the tempo of play and run time off of the clock.
3. The **"76"** which looks like the "70", but with soft pressure and an aggressive corner trap once the ball gets across the half court line.

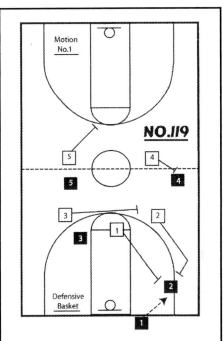

The "80" Press
Motion No.1 (No.119)

On this press you want to tell your players to be aggressive on their play, and force the ball to the sideline and out of the middle of the court. In youth leagues the opponents No.1 (guard) usually inbounds the ball. As soon as they inbound the ball to their No.2 player, your No.1 and No.2 players sprint to their No.2 player and trap them down in the corner. Your No.3

rotates across to the opposite side of the court. Your No.4 rotates over to cover, and "deny" a pass to their No.4 player. Your No.5 player drops back to prevent the long pass for a lay-up. If the opponents No.4 and 5 are switched, then your No.4 and No.5 players switch, with your No.5 covering their tallest player or center. Teach your No.4 and No.5 players to turn their bodies so that they are faced towards the sideline for steals and pass deflections. If they switch and their No.5 takes the ball out, then your No.5 has to not let a speedy guard get behind them. Teach them the CLUE is their No.1 is way up the court.

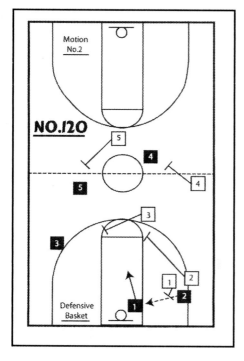

Motion No.2 (No.120)

If the ball is passed back to their No.1, your No.1 slides over a little to "deny" the pass back to their No.2. Your No.3 moves to the middle and waits until your No.2 rotates to the middle, then they slide over to the right side free throw elbow.

Your No.3 does not leave the middle though until your No.2 gets there, to make sure the ball does not get up the middle of the court. Your No.4 and No.5 players rotate back to their starting positions.

Motion No.3 (No.121)

If the ball is reversed to the opposite side of the court, your No.3 has to move over quickly, to block and prevent dribble penetration up the sideline. Your No.1 sprints over to trap, and your No.2 slides over to "deny" the middle pass. Your No.5 slides over to the ball side sideline at half court, to prevent a pass up the sideline.

Your No.4 has to quickly sprint back deep as a safety, to prevent the deep pass and lay-up.

The "70'" Press (No.122)

This is more of a safe press. By that I mean soft pressure, and no trapping. It's safe because there is not much gambling, you don't give up a lay-up, and there is less chance you will foul. The whole object of this version is, slow down the offense, control the tempo, and run some time off the time clock. Your players set up just a few steps deeper than in the "80". Then they just kind of float in front of the player they are guarding, slowing up their progression up the floor.

They keep the ball in front of them, and "deny" any long passes over their head. With one option. If your point guard (No.1) is very fast, quick, and aggressive, have them pressure whoever has the ball, all over the court. Your No.1 sets up first just inside of the top of the key. Your No.2 and No.3 set up just a

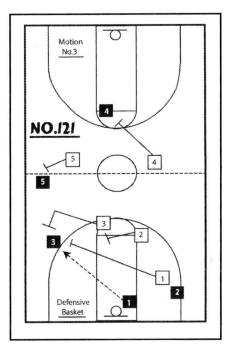

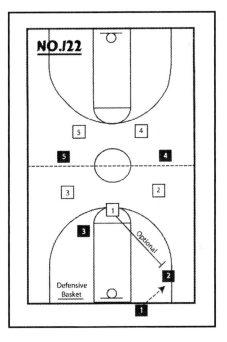

little farther outside of the 3 point arc. Your No.4 and No.5 drop back to just in front of the 3 point arc on their end of the court. Occasionally you can spring a "trap" on them as in version "76". It works well when they think you are just laying back every time.

The "76" Press
Motion No.1 (No.123)

This version starts out like the "70" press with soft pressure. What you do though is, kind of lull them to sleep while your No.1 and No.2 gently steering them over to the sideline trap area. You let them come across court along the side line.

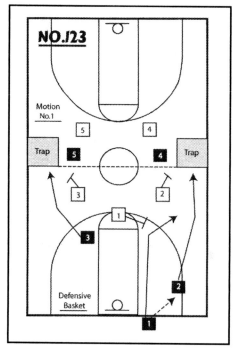

Once they get across the half court line, your No.1 and No.2 players quickly move up and spring the trap on them. However if they come up the other side of the court, you can spring the trap with your No.1 and your No.3 players. Use rules then similar to the "80" press where the opposite side wing No.2 or No.3 denies the pass into the middle area.

To get this play to work, your No.2 and No.3 players will have to do a little "acting". They have to act like they are just not interested in springing a trap. This is to get the ball handler to come up over the half court line into the trap box along the sideline.

The Red "76" Press
Motion No.2 (No.124)

Your No.1, No.2, and No.3 players, depending on which side of the court the ball handler comes up on, trap them in the trap box corner. If the player they have trapped is taller, they will have to get their hands way up to block a lob pass over their heads. Have your trapping players remember, and make sure to keep their legs interlocked.

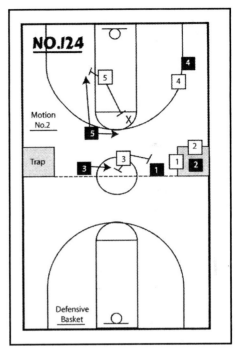

Your opposite wing player No.2 or No.3 "denies" a pass back into the middle, by coming up and pressuring the closest middle of the court player to the trap box. Your No.4 player moves to the sideline to "deny" the pass up the sideline. Your No.5 player moves over to "deny" a pass into the middle area near them. Keeping your No.5 player up near the top of the key is a gamble though because it opens the door, so to speak, for a long diagonal pass over their head to an opponent that has moved under the basket for a shot or lay-up. You probably only want to bring No.5 once in awhile as a surprise tactic.

If you keep doing it every time, eventually you will get beaten by this long pass over the top. I suggest you have a signal with your No.5 player, to let them know when you want them to come up. To make this play work, you are going to have to teach your No.2 and No.3 players to communicate with each other as to what is happening around them. Also teach your No.4 and No.5 players to communicate with each other. They have to "deny" the middle pass out from the trapped player.

A "NOTE" for you coaches that play in a league where they do not let you press. You can still set up at half court, moved back a little, and run this trap play. A little strategy note here. Coaches say there were times when they ran the "70" or "76" play just to get the ball out of the hands of their opponents best player. Then when that happened, they would switch into a "pressure man-to-man" defense, to "deny" the ball back to the opponents best player. Also coaches using this defense say many times, with young youth teams, the offense threw the ball away, and made a turnover because of the pressure and the trap.

Fast Break Transition Defense

The object of this fast break transition defense is, keep the opponent from scoring an easy lay-up, or basket on the fast break. When your team shoots, at least one guard (No.1 or No.2) should not attack the boards and stay back past the 3 point circle, and in the center of the court. My suggestion is assign a certain player or players, to this position, to make sure there is no confusion who will do it.

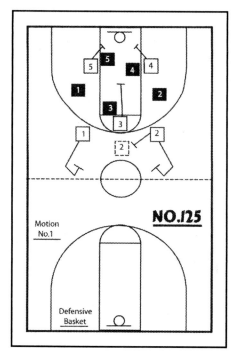

Preventing the Fast Break (No.125)

This is basically the 2 guards back play. Have your No.1 and No.2 players stay back. When a shot goes up your No.3, No.4, and No.5 players "crash" the boards for any rebounds.

Defending the Paint Area after the Break (No.126)

If the offense gets the rebound and starts to come down the court, all your players except your No.1, sprint back down the court to around the paint area, to prevent a quick lay-up by the opposition. Your guard (No.1 or No.2) on the ball side stays back and blocks the dribbler from penetrating, or getting quickly down court. Once the fast break is stopped, all your players can go into their normal man-to-man or zone defense. If your opponent is successful in running a fast break down the court, your prevent guard (No.2) may get caught in a "2 on 1", or a "3 on 1" mismatch match.

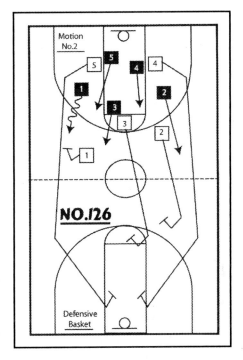

Teach your prevent player to *first* make sure they stop the ball handler from making the lay-up. If the player decides to go for a jump shot, let them take it. It is a lower percentage shot than the lay-up. What they don't want to do is, go out away from the basket and take on the dribbler. This usually lets one of the other players slip behind them, for a pass and an easy lay-up. What they do have to do is "gap" the nearest offensive players, and how they do that is, turn sideways, try to straddle and cut off the passing lanes to the lay-up. If you can get a lot of hustle out of your team, it will stop or slow down the fast break.

Tip Off Defense

There has to be a defense for the "tip off", you can't just ignore it. And even though it only happens a few times a game, you want to get control of the ball. Especially if you are in a championship situation, the game may be close and you want the ball. Even if the team you are playing is taller and stronger, you can still possibly cause them to make a mistake and then quickly get the ball back.

Man-to-Man Pressure "D" (No.127)

Whether they are bigger than you or not, the pressure can cause a turnover. If the offense gets the tip off, it's usually going to go to their No.4 player who is tall. If it does, their No.4 will probably try to pass it off to their No.1 or No.2 out on the wings, to get the ball down the court.

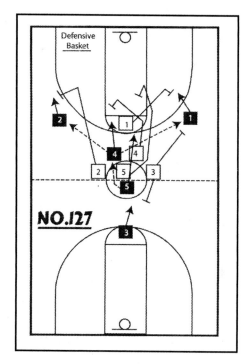

Teach your players to recognize this. The second their No.4 gets the ball, your No.1 sprints out to "deny" their No.1 the pass, or if they do get the pass your No.3 comes over quickly to work a "trap" on them along with your No.1.

Also if the ball goes out to their No.2 on the left wing, your No.1 goes to that side to work a "trap" with your No.2 on them.

If their No.4 holds the ball or dribbles down the lane, your No.4 either goes directly over to pressure them, or sprints down into the lane ahead of them to block them. While all of this is going on, your No.2 sprints over to cover and "deny" their No.2 the pass. Their No.5 center will probably head for the lo-post after tipping to No.4. Your No.5 has to recognize this, and immediately sprint out ahead of their No.5 to "deny" them a pass.

If the tip off goes behind to their No.3 player, your No.3 has to quickly move forward, to block and pressure them from penetrating into the front court. Also make sure to teach your players not to foul the opposing player while they are pressuring them.

Offensive Skill Training Activities (Drills)

ALL DRILLS will be numbered for "EASY" reference.

Offensive drills will cover shooting, dribbling, and passing. We won't have every drill ever invented, but we will pick some of the better ones for little kids, and give you some choices. It is recommended that use of these drills be kept to a 15 minute time limit for the little kids. You can use a whistle to start and stop the drill. Then all players rotate to the next group. You are going to be working them hard so plan for short water breaks periodically every 1/2 hour or so if you have 1.5 hour long practices.

SHOOTING DRILLS

The Bank Shot (No.128)

One player (P1) stands off the left of the basket, the other players line up out to the right of the basket just outside of the 3 point circle. P1 starts with the ball and either bounce passes it or straight passes it to P2 who dribbles to the basket for a lay up. What they have to do though is bank the ball in

every time off the backboard square. Basically they aim for the center of the backboard square. In time they will see that they have to adjust that a little. P1 waits, rebounds, and passes to the next player in the line. Then P1 goes to the end of the line and P2 becomes the new P1. Run the drill fast. At the lower levels this is the most *important* drill to work on for "core memory".

The Baby Jumper Shot (No.129)

The first player in the line passes the ball to P2, who stands with their back to the basket. The pass can be bounce, lob, or straight. P2 whirls around and takes a jump shot into the basket. P1 rebounds. The next player in line moves to P2. While this is happening P1

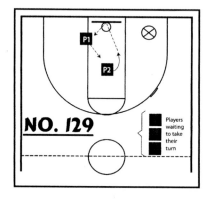

NO. 129

passes to the next player at the front of the line, then moves to the end of the line. P2 moves to the P1 position after shooting, and the old P1 clears out. Then the whole process starts over again with the front player in the line passing to P2. Make sure P2 gets way up in the air on their jump shot. Run the drill fast.

Beginners Lay on the Floor (No.130)

This is a real simple lay on the floor, push the ball straight up, catch it with only one hand, and push it back up again. If there are 5 in the group they can all lay on their backs in a circle, heads to the outside, with the coach in the middle observing. Have them push the ball straight up 5 times with each hand, and without dropping it. Rest a few minutes the do another 5 pushes.

Beginners sit on the Chair (No.131)

This is a real simple sit in the chair drill, face the basket, push the ball straight up into the basket, using only a one hand set shot. Coach is under the basket passing rebounds back to player, observes, and gives instructions. Start out with chair only 6 to 8 feet away, and move back towards free throw line a little each time as they get better and older. If there are 5 in the group they can line up behind the chair. Have them push the ball straight up to the basket 5 times with only the one hand and then the other. Then rotate and the next player takes 10 shots. This builds up their strength to the basket. Make sure they line up their elbow and do the "goose neck" follow through correctly.

Around the Chair Screen (No.132)

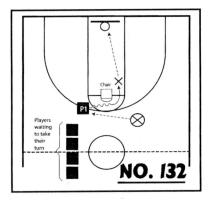

This is a real simple set up the screen around the chair drill, square up to the basket, take the short jumper up into the basket, using only a one hand set shot. P1 starts to move around the chair. Coach makes a bounce pass to them. They dribble just around the chair, then stop and make a baby jumper shot. Then they get their own rebound and pass the ball back to the coach. Then they go to the end of the line, and the coach passes the ball to a new P1. The chair is just there to act as a screener for the shot. Make sure they line up their elbow and do the "goose neck" follow through correctly.

The Knockout Game (No.133)

This is an elimination game. The last one left wins. Players P1, P2, P3 have a basketball and stand in a line about 6 to 8 feet out in front of the basket. P1 shoots. If they make the shot they pass

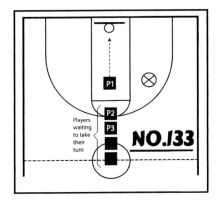

the ball to the 3rd player in the line, then go to the end of the line. If they miss they rebound and try to make a basket as quickly as possible. P2 can move up to the starting point and make their shot as soon as P1 takes their shot. If P1 misses their shot and P2 makes their shot before P1 is able to rebound and make a basket, then P1 is eliminated.

85

P2 must make their shot before P3, P4, or P5. Play keeps going until only one player is left. In other words if a player makes their shot before the player ahead of them, they eliminate that player.

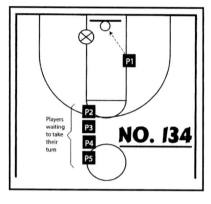

The H.O.R.S.E. Game (No.134)

This is an elimination game. The last player left after everyone has been labeled with the word wins. Establish a player shooting order. The coach can call the type of shot and location or it can be players choice. P1 starts and takes a shot. If they make the shot, every player after them has to make the same exact shot in type and location. The player who misses is labeled with an "H". On your second miss, you get an "O", and so on until you have been labeled with H-O-R-S-E. After a miss the next player can introduce a new shot that everyone has to make. If all the players make the shot in the round, the next player gets to start a new shot. Keep the game moving fast for thew best results.

DRIBBLING DRILLS

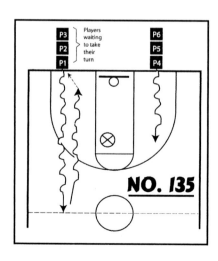

Controlled Half Court Dribbling (No.135)

Your team is divided into two groups lined up on the base line. The little kids go half court and the bigger kids full court. Have both P1 and P4 first "power" dribble down to the half court line (or full court) and then back going as fast as they can. When they get almost back they pass the ball of to the next player in line who dribbles down and back. When it gets back to P1 and P4 again they "cross over" dribble down and back the next time. Then "stop-N-go", and then "switch hands" the next time. Right handers use their left hand and left handers their right hand. Keep the drill moving so that each player gets to go down and back at least once with each of the 4 types of dribbling.

Weave Switch Dribbling (No.136)

Your team is divided into two groups lined up on the base line. The little kids go half court and the bigger kids full court. This is just like drill No.135 except the players weave around chairs staggered out in front of them. As they go around each chair to a different side they cross

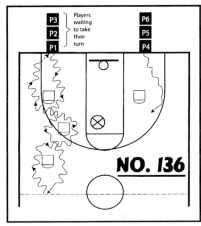

over and switch hands so that the dribble hand is always the hand away from the chair. They dribble down to the half court line for the little kids and full court for the bigger kids. Keep the drill moving so that each player gets to go down and back at least 3 or 4 times. You can walk the little kids through it at first then speed it up little by little as they get better. The goal is to get everyone running it fast. Use as many folding chairs as you need. If you can't find chairs use other players or coaches standing still. Or you can just have one line if you are short chairs, players, and coaches.

Man to Man Zigzag Dribbling (No.137)

Have your players pair off along the side of the court. On one side is the dribblers (P1,P2) with the ball. Opposite of them are the defenders (P3,P4).

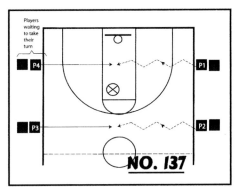

There are 3 speeds to this drill. Walking, half speed, and full speed. P1 and P2 zigzag dribble from sideline to sideline. P3 and P4 move right straight at them at the same speed. As they meet P3 and P4 uses a defensive stance and tries to force the P1 and P2 to go around them, shuffling back and forth. They have to stay right with the P1 and P2 as they zig and zag across court. P3 and P4 can't steal the ball and the P1 and P2 can't run into them or blow past them. When they all reach the far side sideline they switch positions. P3 and P4's job is to just keep themselves between P1 or P2 and the sideline behind them. If P1 or P2 beats P3 or P4, then they have to turn around, sprint back and get in front of the them again. This is called a "turn and go". When they get to a full speed run P1 and P2 still have to zig and zag their way across court. Run a walk through first, then a half speed, then a full speed.

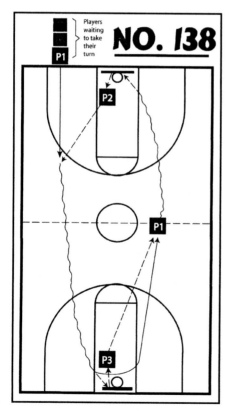

Full Court Throw and Go Dribbling (No.138)

Have your players line up at one end of the court. 2 players P2 and P3 go to a low post position under the basket. The first player P1 starts running down the court. P2 throws them the basketball when they are about 1/3 of the way down the court. The throw has to be a little ahead of them so that they can catch it without slowing down.

P1 gets the ball and starts dribbling fast break style and goes in for a lay-up. They then turn and fast break back up the court to the basket on the other end. P3 gets the rebound then throws a long outlet pass to

P1 breaking down court the other way. P1 gets the ball again and starts dribbling fast break style, then they go in for another lay-up. After that they go to the end of the line. P2 gets the rebound, then the next player in line starts a fast break down the court.

The object is for the shooter to try and make the lay-up, and for P2 and P3 to jump up and get the rebound. After each player gets 3 fast breaks down the court and back, rotate P2 and P3 so that they get a chance to get their 3 fast breaks. And 2 new P2 and P3's get to work on their rebounding. If the lay-up misses emphasize to the rebounders that they have to jump up and gab the rebound off the backboard. Not to just stand there and wait for it to come down.

PASSING DRILLS

Against the Wall (No.139)

Have your players line up in front of one of the gym walls. 10 to 12 feet for the little kids, about 15 feet for the bigger kids. First have them make a "chest" pass, then a "bounce" pass, then a "one handed" pass, and last an "overhead" pass.

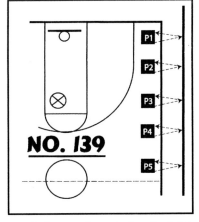

Each player should make at least 5 each of all four passes. The chest pass should hit the wall or reach the receiver at chest height. The bounce pass should hit the floor about 2/3's of the way between the thrower and the wall or receiver. The one handed pass should hit the wall or reach the receiver at chest height.

The overhead pass should hit the wall or reach the receiver at about head to shoulder height. Emphasize that they should learn to pass first stepping out with their left foot, then their right foot. Also make sure they snap their wrists, step into their passes, and focus their eyes on where they are throwing ball to. As an *alternative* they can line up facing a partner and do this drill. This makes a good warm-up drill

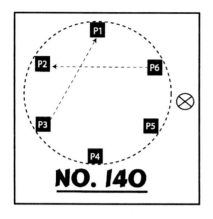

NO. 140

Circular in Traffic Passing (No.140)

Have your players line up in a big circle at center court, at least arms width apart. Give 2 players a basketball that are opposite of each other in the circle. The coach stands outside of the circle with a whistle. When the whistle is blown the 2 players with the ball make a "chest" pass to another player on the other side of the circle.

Then that player makes a pass to another player opposite of them and so on. They keep doing this until you blow your whistle in about 3 minutes. The object is keep passing the ball to another opposite player without the ball hitting the ground, and without the 2 balls hitting each other. Emphasize to them do not try to make a team mate miss because they think it's funny. This is not how to promote good team work. Then blow your whistle and for the next 3 minutes they make "bounce" passes. Follow that with 3 minutes of "one hand" passes, then 3 minutes of "overhead" passes.

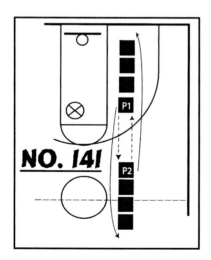

NO. 141

Line Passing (No.141)

Have your players line up in 2 lines near center court and the free throw line facing each other about 12 to 15 feet apart. Each player has a basketball. Player P1 passes their ball to P2 then goes to the end of P2's line. P2 passes their ball to the next player behind P1, then goes to the end of P1's line.

The player catching P2's ball passes their ball to the player behind P2, then goes to the end of P2's line and so on until player P1 and P2 get to the front of the lines again. Then they change the type of pass. Start out with everyone making a "chest" pass, then they all go to a "bounce" pass, then a "one handed" pass, and last an "overhead" pass. Some of the time have them fake to the right then to left before passing straight ahead.

Star Passing (No.142

Have your players line up in a 5 point star formation at center court about 12 to 15 apart from their passing partner. Player P1 passes their ball to P2 then goes to the end of P2's line. P2 passes their ball to P3 and then goes to the end of P3's line. P3 to P4 and so on until player P1 get to the front of the line again.

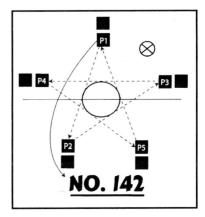

Then they change the type of pass. Start out with everyone making a "chest" pass, then they all go to a "bounce" pass, then a "one handed" pass, and last an "overhead" pass. This is another drill that is great to use for part of your warm-up before the game. In other words follow your pass and go to the end of that line. Work on this until your players can really run this drill fast because it looks really cool. This won't work very well unless you have at least 10 players though. You can run this drill with a 3 point star if you only have only 6 players available.

Secondary Break Passing/ Shooting (No.143)

Have your players break up into 2 half court groups. Have them get into 2 lines on each half court. One on the right wing, and one near the center circle. P1 takes the ball and dribbles towards the top of the key, stops, and passes to

91

P2 on the right wing who has started to run towards the basket. P2 catches the pass, comes under control then takes a jump shot at the basket. Then they quickly follow their shot in, get the rebound, pass the ball back to the next player in line at center court. Then they go to end of the P2 line. A new player takes the ball, dribbles up, and passes the ball to the next player in the P2 line who has started a run towards the basket. Then the process keeps going until each player has made at least 3 passes and shots. Then the shooting line moves over the left wing and the process starts again. Try to keep the lines small so that the drill keeps moving.

Defensive Skill Training Activities (Drills)

ALL DRILLS will be numbered for "EASY" reference.

Defensive drills will cover guarding, stealing, rebounding, and shot blocking. We won't have every drill ever invented, but we will pick some of the better ones for little kids, and give you some choices. It is recommended that use of these drills be kept to a 15 minute time limit for the little kids. You can use a whistle to start and stop the drill. Then all players rotate to the next group. You are going to be working them hard so plan for short water breaks periodically every 1/2 hour or so if you have 1.5 hour long practices.

GUARDING DRILLS

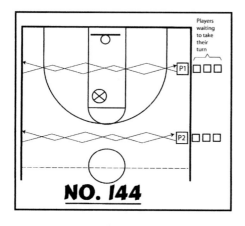

NO. 144

Sideline to Sideline Shuffle/Slide (No.144)
Have your players line up on one side of the half court in 2 lines. The front players P1 and P2 get into their defensive stance and start slide shuffling sideways across the court. The object is to stay low all the way

across and back, then go to the end of the line. They keep their arms held out wide, and they have to slap the floor about every 3 steps with both hands. This is core training to teach their body to stay low. Depending on their age and how many players you have you may only want to run this drill for 5 to 10 minutes. And you may want to run this drill just to center court and back for the little kids. It's a draining drill so that should be enough for them.

Guarding the Dribbler (No.145)

Have your players line up on both sides of the half court in 2 lines. The front players P1, P3, have the basketball. The players P2, P4, on the other side are the defenders. To

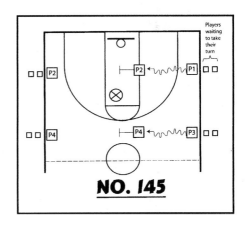

NO. 145

start P2, P4 go over and get right in front of P1, P3, about 10 feet away and get into their defensive stance. P1 starts a zigzag dribble across the court. P2, P4, have to stay right in front of them while shuffling sideways and moving backwards, and they can't touch P1 or P3. P1, P3, just keeps advancing and dribbling while turning a little sideways and dribbling with the backside hand when they get too close. The object is for P2, P4, to stay right in front of P1, P3, while they maintain a 2 or 3 foot distance. For the real little kids you can run the drill only half way from center court.

Guarding the Shooter (No.146)

Have your players line up in 2 groups.

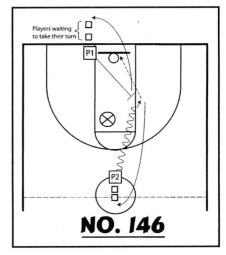

NO. 146

One at end of the court under the basket and the other at center court. P1 is the defender and P2 is the shooter with the ball. On the whistle P2 tries to dribble in and make a basket. P1 comes out to stop them. P2 can try a jump shot, or they can try to dribble around P1 and go for a lay-up. P2 can not charge into P1, they have to try and go around. If they run into P1 the drill is dead and they each stop and go to end of line. After each player has had at least 3 turns then rotate the groups so that all players get a chance to shoot and defend. This drill is run just like a game situation. P1 can't reach in and foul, or the drill stops and both players go back to the end of the line. Blow your whistle on fouls and charging.

STEALING DRILLS

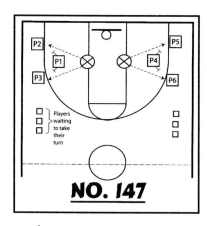

Stealing the Pass (No.147)

Have your players line up in 2 groups. You can run this drill out on the two wings where there is room. You have the ball coach. P1 and P4 are the players trying to steal the pass. It's kind of a game of keep away. P2, P3, P5, and P6 are the pass receivers. Give yourself 5 to 10 seconds then throw the pass to either receiver.

The receivers have to stay in the same position. The pass stealers have to watch your hands and attempt to intercept the ball as it comes out. The receivers should start out about 10 feet apart to make it easier. When P1, P4, get better then spread them out farther, and fake the pass some of the time. After about 3 attempts rotate the ball stealers. After all the players have had a chance to make a steal then rotate them with the receivers.

Stealing the Dribblers Ball (No.148)

This is almost like Drill 145, except the defender can go for the ball. It's very hard to learn without fouling, but the little kids have to start somewhere. What this drill will teach them is core memory for reaching for the ball. On your whistle P1 and P3 try to dribble the ball to the other side of the court. P2 and P4 go out and intercept them and attempt to steal the ball. P1 and P3 protect the ball and try to get around P2 and P4.

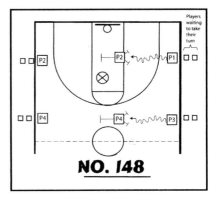

NO. 148

The rule is they can't move more than 5 feet to either side as they go across. What P2 and P4 have to do is watch the ball as they get close. They have to keep sliding and backing up. They can not touch any part of the dribbler's body if they reach in. As the dribbler moves forward they wait their chance then go for the ball and try to grab it with both hands for a held ball, or knock it away without hitting the dribblers hands. If P1 or P3 make it to the other side they give the ball to the next player in the line on that side. Then they switch and the dribblers go from that side.

REBOUNDING DRILLS

Beginners Rebounding (No.149)

This is a simple beginners rebounding drill. Have your players line up in 2 groups at the end line. P1 and P2 go under the basket on each side. You stand in front of the basket with the ball. On your signal you throw up a shot that does not go through the basket. Whichever side the ball rebounds to, that player has to time their jump so that they go up in the air and grab the rebound over their head and before it hits the floor.

Back away from the basket after your shot in case

NO. 149

the rebound goes right out in front of the basket. In that case both players have to move over and fight for the rebound. When the rebound is caught or the ball hits the floor the drill is dead. And both players go to the end of the line on the opposite side. By going to the end of the other line the players automatically rotate themselves.

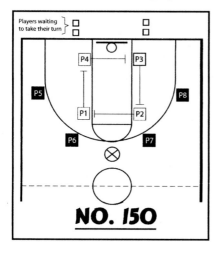

Circle the Wagons (No.150)

Have your players line up in 2 groups at the end line. One group is offense and the other is defense. This is a 4 on 4 drill. P1- P4 slowly rotate around clockwise in a square around the free throw lane. As they move around you throw the ball at the basket. P1 - P4 have to match up with P5, P6, P7, or P8 depending on which one is closest to them as they rotate around the square.

Then when the shot from the coach goes up they box them out and try to get the rebound. P5- P8 can grab, push, or do anything they want to try to get the ball. The object is to teach them defensive rebounding. The defense tries to get 3 straight rebounds. If they miss a rebound before getting 3 straight, they have to start over at zero or they have to run suicides. After that switch or rotate the offense and defense.

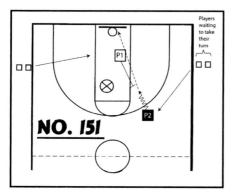

One on One Rebounding (No.151)

Have your players line up in 2 groups at each sideline. One group is offense and the other is defense. P2 goes anywhere out on the perimeter, takes only 2 dribbles then takes a perimeter shot. P2 can not attempt to drive past P1. When they start to dribble P1 goes out to meet them, and raises their hands in front of them as P2 takes the shot. After the shot P1 boxes out P2 by making butt contact.

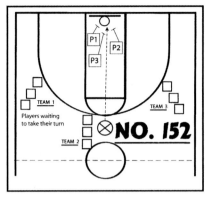

They make whatever moves they have to, go right or left, step in the path, hold their position, maintain contact, and look for the ball. Make sure they hustle to pursue the ball. P2 has to try for the rebound also. Have them make 3 tries then rotate the players.

Dan Maria Rebounding Drill (No.152)

This is a special former coaches drill for rebounding. You split your team up into 3 groups or teams. Each has to have an equal number of players. Each team lines up outside the 3 point circle, and send 1 representative into the 3 second lane (paint). You take a shot at the basket. Whoever gets the rebound returns it to the coach. That player goes to the end of their team's line, and the next player from that line goes into the paint. The players from the other 2 teams stay in the paint until they get a rebound. The first team to have all it's players get a rebound wins. Then the other 2 teams get to run suicides.

Manhattan College Drill (No.153)

This is another special former coaches drill for rebounding. This is a drill for the bigger kids, not the little kids. This lets you know who your real scrappy kids are. It's a little too rough for the beginners. You have the

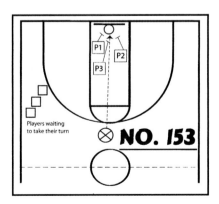

97

ball at the foul line. If you have another coach and enough players you can split into 2 groups at each end of the court. Put 3 players in the paint. You shoot the ball at the basket. All 3 players try for the rebound. Whoever gets the rebound attempts to shoot a basket. The other 2 players are allowed to foul the rebounder to keep them from scoring. However it can't be a flagrant foul, but they should be physical. When one of the players makes their basket, the ball becomes live again as soon as it goes through the net. The first player that scores 3 times gets to go out, then a new player joins the other remaining 2. The remaining 2 start back at zero baskets (scores). This drill teaches toughness. This goes continuous because the ball is always live, so 10 minutes of this and the remaining players that can't score are "gassed".

SHOT BLOCKING

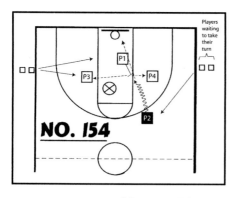

One on One Shot Blocking (No.154)

Have your players line up in 2 groups at each sideline. One group is offense and the other is defense. P2 goes anywhere out on the perimeter, takes only 4 dribbles then has to make a perimeter jump shot. P2 can not attempt to drive past P1.

When they start to dribble P1 goes out to meet them. They have to watch very carefully to time their block. They can block the shot just as P2 starts to bring it up to shoot and it's still in their hand, or they can try to block it in the air as it comes off P2's hand. What they have to learn to do is block it and push it to either P3 or P4 as opposed to swatting it out of bounds. After 3 blocks rotate all players. Make sure your taller centers and forwards always get their attempts in.

98

Team Games

These are games you can have your team play once in a while. This will break up the practice from endless drills. The kids are learning a skill, but having a little fun.

The Bean Bag Game (No.155)

This game will help your players develop good dribbling skills. Split up into three teams. This is a half court game. Put one team at center court. The other two teams go to the two corners of the base line. Each team has one ball. Place ten or twelve bean bags in a pile in the key circle. On your command one player from each team dribbles into the key circle, then while still dribbling each

player reaches down and picks up a bean bag. Next they dribble back to their team and while still dribbling they deposit the bean bag.

Then they give the ball to the next team member who dribbles out to pick up another bean bag. The RULE is they can only take one bean

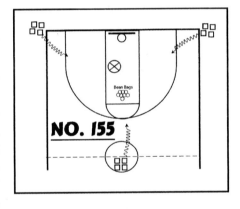

bag at a time. This keeps going on until all the bean bags in the circle are gone. After that they can dribble over and steal the other teams bean bags. Waiting players can not stop them from stealing. After two minutes of play the team with the most bean bags wins

The Ball Scramble Game (No.156)

This game will help your players develop their skills for getting to loose balls, learning to move quickly without the ball. Give all your players a ball and send them to the key circle in the middle of half court. On your command they all drop their ball and run to the half court center line or the bleachers or wherever you want to send them. They touch there and run back to the key circle. While

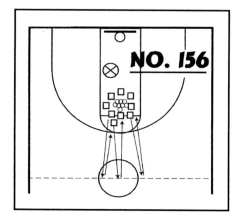

the players are running you remove one ball. The player without a ball is out of the game. On your command it starts over. With fewer players reduce the area. Last player with a ball wins the game.

The Obstacle Course Relay Game (No.157)

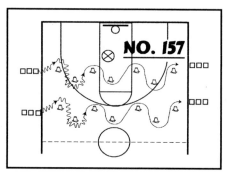

This is a game that will help your players develop their skills to dribble around opponent's. Split up into two teams. Put half on one side of the court, and half on the other side. This is a relay race. On your command the front player on both teams starts weave dribbling around each cone to the other side line. When they have passed the side line (A RULE) they hand off to their team mate on that side. No cheating and passing to the team mate. The team mate dribbles back through the course and hands off to the next team mate. This can go on for ten minutes. Whichever team is ahead wins the game.

The "HORSE" Game (No.158)

This is a fun game that will help your players with their shooting accuracy. You can adapt it for your team. Line up all your players at the half court line. You will probably need a note book to keep track of the letters each player has. The first player tries to make a shot, any kind they like. Then they go to the end of the line. If the second player makes the exact same shot then they go to the end of the line. If they miss the shot they get a letter "H." After a miss the next player in line gets to pick their shot. It keeps going until there is a miss. That player gets the next letter until the word "H-O-R-S-E" is spelled out. When a player gets all the letters then they are out of the game. The last player left without all the letters wins the game.

The "Around the World" Game (No.159)

This is a game to help your players with their shot accuracy and their shot distance. Take a pieces of tape and mark them with all the letters. Put the tape pieces at each letter spot. Split your team up into groups of three.

Each group has a basketball. Players can attempt two shots from each letter. They start at "A" and go around to the

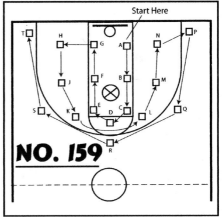

next letter. If they make the shot then they can move to the next letter and continue shooting. If a player misses their first attempt, they can elect to stop at that spot then give the ball to the next shooter on the following team. They start at that spot when it is their next turn.If they elet to shoot the second shot and miss it, they give the ball up to the next shooter. On their next turn they go back and start over at spot "A." The first player to go all the way around to the last letter ("T") wins the game

If it's too EASY there are variations. After going all the way to the top letter, have players return in reverse order. Have players use their right arm, then the left, on every other shot Have players use only their weak arm (left). The backboard must always be used.

The Steal the Bacon Game (No.160)

This is a little game you can play to help your players learn to protect and shield the ball, and to make steals. You can play this game 2 vs 1 or 1 vs 1, or both ways (best). Line your team up back at the at the half court line. Your first player goes to the top of the key with a basketball. Then one or two defenders go to the edges of the lane.

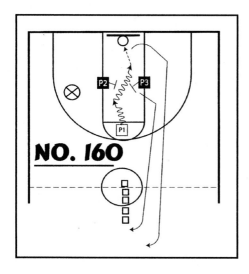

On your whistle P1 has one minute to dribble through the defenders and attempt to take a shot at the basket. Blow your whistle after one minute is up. You may need to go to two minutes for the real little kids. If P1 can't break through the two players then go 1 vs 1 (P1,P2).

If P1 can break through, give them one point. If they make the basket, give them two points. Have one of your assistant coaches keep score in a notebook. If P2 or P3 can steal the ball cleanly, give them two points. If they can knock the ball away, give them one point. However, they can not touch the dribblers arms at any point in the attempt. Make sure that everyone gets a chance to play the offensive and defensive positions. The player with the most points wins the game.

I would play the game no longer than one hour then move on to someting else. Here is an idea. Break your team up into two groups. The other group can be working on something else at the other end of the court. This way everyone keeps busy and you get more teaching in.

102